PHIL RIZZUTO:
A Yankee Tradition

Dan Hirshberg

SAGAMORE PUBLISHING
Champaign, Illinois

Production Manager: Susan M. McKinney
Dustjacket and photo insert design: Michelle R. Dressen
Editor: David Hamburg
Proofreader: Phyllis L. Bannon

The New York Yankees' photographs of Phil Rizzuto were reproduced with the permission of the New York Yankees.

Publisher's Cataloging in Publication
(prepared by Quality Books Inc.)

Hirshberg, Daniel L.
Phil Rizzuto: a Yankee tradition/ Daniel Hirshberg.
p. cm.
Includes index.
Preassigned LCCN: 92-63140
ISBN 0-915611-71-6

      1. Rizzuto, Phil, 1918- 2. Baseball players—United States—
Biography. I. Title.

GV865.R5H57 1993   796.357'092
                                QBI93-931

Printed in the United States

*To my wife Susan, and my children Nathan and Melanie.
You guys are the best family in the world.*

———————————◆———————————

Contents

Acknowledgments vi
Preface viii
Foreword xii

1 A Budding Ball Player 1

2 A Minor League Star 15

3 Welcome to the Big Time 29

4 Rookie Rizzuto 41

5 Reflections on a Rookie Year 61

6 War Beckons 73

7 Five in a Row 93

8 A Career Winds Down 117

9 To the Booth 135

10 A True Friend 149

11 "My Life is Not Complete" 163

12 Reflections 183

Index 193

Acknowledgments

As with any book, the author can do only so much on his or her own. This book was no different. Without the help of others, *Phil Rizzuto: A Yankee Tradition*, would not be a reality. I have to give credit where credit belongs.

Many thanks to the following individuals: Anthony Schillizzi, an associate of Phil Rizzuto; he helped to clarify many Scooter stories and offered me assistance when I needed it; Helen Stiles and Bill Dean of the National Baseball Hall of Fame Library, who were a big help in gaining access to quite a bit of information on the Scooter (he may not be a Hall of Famer, but he does have a bulging file in the library); Dr. Anthony Serafini, who clued me in to the book game; John Fenimore, my unofficial editor; Dr. Ron Sultan, my confidant during stressful times; Jerry Karp, whose loyal friendship was greatly appreciated when it was needed most; Bill Deeter, who allowed me flexibility during a crazy time of year; my wife Susan and my two children, Nathan and Melanie, who put up with a grump during deadline pressure; the scores of former Yankees, former Yankee opponents, and Yankee officials who were cooperative during my interviews; and people like Sid Bordman and Ed Lucas, whose personal relationships with Phil Rizzuto were described to me in frank detail.

And thanks to Emery Konick of the New Jersey Sportswriters Association; to Jim Ogle, who heads the Yankee Alumni Association; to former *Star-Gazette* writer Monica Fernandez, who went beyond the call of duty developing photos for me; to Arlene Schulman, whose support and help was appreciated; to the Yankee public relations department, which offered assistance when I needed it; to the people at the Hackettstown and Centenary libraries; to Steve Gietschier of *The Sporting News*, for giving me guidance in regard to copyright law; to the many writers, past and present, whose legwork in years past helped to make this book a complete Phil Rizzuto package; and to everyone else whose lives touched mine as I researched and wrote this book.

Special thanks to Joe Bannon Sr. and Joe Bannon Jr. of Sagamore Publishing, who gave me the opportunity to do this book in the first place.

Thank you one and all.

Preface

It was the fall of 1974. I was a freshman at Stockton State College in Pomona, New Jersey back then; a recent graduate of Columbia High School in Maplewood, New Jersey. At that time I was concerned about where the next party was, not about baseball. In fact, there are a couple of years there where I draw a complete blank when it comes to baseball. Other years I can tell you who led the league in hitting, who won more games. But in the fall of 1974, quite frankly, I couldn't have cared less about our national pastime. I do remember one thing about 1974, though. Mickey Hirshberg, my father, came home one evening and reported that he'd met Phil Rizzuto that morning. Seems the Scooter was on his way to the dentist. My father's grocery store, H&M Market, on Elmora Avenue in Elizabeth, was along the route from Rizzuto's home in Hillside to the dentist. Rizzuto ordered a cup of coffee and chatted with my father about the recent blockbuster trade that sent Bobby Murcer to the San Francisco Giants for slugging Bobby Bonds. "He was in no hurry to get to the dentist," my father said. "He was very nice, very personable. We talked about the trade and what it meant to the Yankees." Rizzuto stopped in a few more times, ordering coffee and chatting with my father. I recall wishing I had been there, too,

What did I know of Phil Rizzuto? Not much, really. I listened to him broadcast Yankee games on radio and television, knew he was a bit excitable, and always heard him congratulating somebody for something or other on the air. I certainly never saw Rizzuto play ball. I'd heard he was a pretty good bunter and could field with anybody. In the late 1960s, when Strat-O-Matic was big-time in my neighborhood (actually, still is around my house), I remember participating in a marathon Strat-O-Matic baseball afternoon at the home of Ed Mills. It was Ed, Jerry "Rocky" Karp (his outfield play in stickball behind Clinton School earned him the nickname made famous by Ron Swoboda),

Eddie Sacher, soon to be O.J. Sacher, and more recently, Dallas Sacher, and me that day. Maybe Mike Chaplowitz was there, too. Mills had no current "Strat" teams, just selected old-time great teams. There, among the pile, was the 1941 New York Yankees. How did I know this was Rizzuto's rookie season? I didn't. I only knew that it was a damn good Yankee team and that Rizzuto was part of it. I had no clue that manager Joe McCarthy benched the shortstop for an extended period early in the year. I did know that Rizzuto was somebody special. If, for no other reason, because he was on television. But he was my starting shortstop that day, and any other time I got to "manage" that '41 club. He was my leadoff hitter. And the more I used him, the more I realized he was a good ball player, an excellent fielder, and that he was much more than just some guy announcing the ball-and-strike count.

The first time I personally "interacted" with Phil Rizzuto was during the strike-shortened 1981 season. I was working for the *Daily Record* out of Parsippany, New Jersey. I was given my first professional baseball assignment in May. I was to interview Rickey Henderson of the Oakland A's for a feature story about his days as a minor leaguer in Jersey City, New Jersey. Later, on the elevator to the press box, the doors opened in between levels. There before me on a pay telephone was Phil Rizzuto. "Hi, it's the Scooter," he said with a smile. The elevator doors shut on this surrealistic experience.

Another time, I was waiting for the elevator at Yankee Stadium when I heard someone behind me. "You've got to stand back here." I looked back and it was Phil Rizzuto. "There's two elevators and this is the only way to know which one is coming next," he said. It was a day game that afternoon, and Phil told me that "in his time, we always played day games." Could've been my Uncle Morris talking about his ice cream route in Newark.

What I hadn't known about Phil, I learned through my research with this book. Even though Phil did not want to be a participant in the writing of this book, his friends and former teammates were happy to be interviewed. What came across during the course of the interviews was a genuine love for this man, this person who to many other people, is the guy who, for so many years, pushed "The Money Store" on television. "The Money Store" hired Phil when it had just one office. Now, it is

ix

located worldwide, and is a multimillion-dollar operation. Until recently, when former major league star Jim Palmer replaced him, Rizzuto was the company's sole spokesman. Contrary to what some people believe, Rizzuto does not own The Money Store. He probably wishes he did.

The Rizzuto you see on Yankee broadcasts, the one you hear doing media interviews, is the real Rizzuto. This is one former player who remains loyal to his fans. Of course, as a player, he was a loyal person as well. Over the years he has never forgotten his roots. He knows where he came from, and knows where he wants to go. Whether he's in the supermarket, at a flower shop, or at Yankee Stadium, Phil is Phil. What you see is what you get. And it's wonderful.

"He's the name," says Yankee general manager Gene Michael. "He is the guy. He's been around so long and he's kept his sense of humor. I hope that when I'm his age I can have the same sense of humor. I hope I feel about things the way he does."

"Phil is just a super person," adds former teammate Gil McDougald. "Everybody loves him."

"Phil is still nice to everybody," says former Yankee Allie Clark. "He is always nice, always has a nice word for everybody. Always has a hello and a smile on his face. He's always ready to help somebody if they need it."

In order to capture the life of Phil Rizzuto, I have used portions of many magazine and newspaper articles. There was often confusion about where Rizzuto grew up, and that confusion may come across when reading a segment of an article. He was born in Brooklyn and spent his teenage years in Queens, close to the Brooklyn border. He never lived on Long Island. There are also many stories about Phil, as you can imagine. However, rarely is one story without two versions. Efforts have been made to ascertain the real one, and in many cases, offer the second version.

What I hope you will get from this book is that Phil Rizzuto, a celebrity in these times, was a celebrity in those times. In his hometown of Hillside he has always been involved with community events, one time participating in a panel discussion at the high school about the "Psychology of Raising Our Children." He appeared on "What's My Line," "The Ed Sullivan

Show," and other television shows of the time. These days, late-night TV show host David Letterman and morning shock DJ Howard Stern have made every effort to lure Rizzuto into appearing on their shows. Phil, perhaps wisely, has refused.

Only Phil Rizzuto could have his broadcast banter turned into poetry in the *Village Voice*. Only Phil Rizzuto could end up a rock star with Meat Loaf, and not realize it until the record was out. Only Phil Rizzuto could get away with beating the Stadium traffic for so many years while his partners in the booth were left behind, wondering how long it would be until they got home.

This is the story of Phil Rizzuto, the last link between the Yankee past and the Yankee present. This is Phil Rizzuto, a Yankee tradition . . . and then some.

Foreword

When I was nine years old, a group of us went to Yankee Stadium for a game. It was thrilling. It was like a magnificent temple. It was as great a feeling as when I made my debut at the Met in 1945. I'll never forget seeing Babe Ruth and all the other Yankee greats that day. It was a tremendous experience, especially for a kid from Brooklyn who had only seen Ebbets Field.

It's been an equally tremendous experience knowing Phil Rizzuto. I went to so many Yankee games over the years and to me, he was one of the best shortstops in the business. I loved to watch him play. Like a fine opera singer, he could hit the high note on the field with precision.

For more than twenty years, I have been singing the National Anthem on Opening Day and other special occasions at the stadium. The first time I did it I was more nervous than when I sang in London before the Queen. During these 20 or so years I have become good friends with Phil. He has a wonderful sense of humor. I have never heard anybody say a negative thing about the guy. Some guys you say, he's all right, but he can be self-centered, or he can be mean. Not Phil.

All this fame, people writing about him, talking about him. It hasn't affected him. Through it all he's remained a simple, ordinary character. And I don't think I've ever seen him get angry. Oh, maybe for a second or two. But then he calms down right away. It never lasts. He is a real human being. And a family man. He has a lovely wife, Cora. They are very much in love. Phil is very straightlaced. There have never been rumors about his personal life. I admire that. He is a man with a great deal of pride.

When he talks about friends on the air, there is a sincerity to it. When Phil sends his greetings, or other messages, he means it. He doesn't just do it to fulfill an obligation. He really feels it.

He's a very sensitive man in many ways. He loves kids. He'll stand there and sign autographs for kids and adults. It doesn't bother him like it does some other athletes. He'll stop and talk to anybody. There have been times I'll be walking out of the stadium with him and he's anxious to get home, but he'll stand and talk to the fans. I admire that very much.

I have so many memories of Phil.

When I threw out the first ball a couple of years ago on opening day I was wearing my uniform No. 1 1/2 — which he kids me about all the time — and after a big introduction, I got ready to throw the ball from the pitcher's mound. I was very nervous. I cheated. I moved in about 20 feet. Finally, I threw the ball. Thank God. Now the boys in the booth were trying to figure out how fast it was. Bill White said, "Oh, maybe 20 miles an hour." You know what my friend Phil said, "Two days!"

Then there was the time they had Phil Rizzuto Day. That was in 1985. I thought Phil was going to faint when I asked him to sing the National Anthem with me. Later, among the gifts he got, they gave him a cow. Well, the cow knocks him over. I was standing there right next to him because I had sang the National Anthem and picked him up. That was really funny.

I've invited him to the opera many times. He'll say yes, and then he backs out. I think he feels he wouldn't know what it is about. He'll be interested, then tell me he doesn't think he'd fit in!

I used to take Billy Martin and Phil out to play golf with me at the Westchester Country Club. I wish I had filmed the matches. Billy Martin would, on every hole, have something to say to Phil. "Watch it Phil, now watch your backswing. Keep your head down." And he would drive him nuts. One time we were putting and Phil was about to putt and a fly flew right on Phil's ball. Phil was trying to push it away and Billy said if you push it away you're going to lose the hole. What an experience with those two. What fun. The patience Phil had with Billy. He could take it. Of course, he loved Billy.

When Mike Pagliarulo first came up they were pronouncing his name a couple of different ways, with the G sound, and with a silent G. Phil called me, wanted to know how to pronounce it since I could speak Italian. I told him with the silent G. He was cute, he said you're with the opera so that's what I'll call him. What impressed me was that he was interested in doing it right.

Oh, there are so many other stories and memories of Phil. There are so many wonderful memories.

As far as the Hall of Fame goes, he deserves to be in there. The great-hitting Ted Williams said that if the Boston Red Sox had Phil Rizzuto all those years, it would have been the Sox, not the Yankees, who won all those pennants. Williams meant it, too. The Hall of Fame people have asked me to sing the National Anthem up there several times. But I won't do it. Not until Phil is in there.

My dream was to be a ball player. I played semi-pro ball with Tommy Holmes in Brooklyn. Eventually I got into the opera. I made my debut at the Met in 1945. I was there for 34 years, giving almost 800 performances. Between seeing him on the field, and listening to him on the air, I've seen or heard Phil Rizzuto give at least 800 performances. In my book, he was a star in each and every one.

—Robert Merrill

"During one game, announcer Bill White eyed Rizzuto's new navy blue tie with yellow silhouettes. 'Phil,' said White, 'You've got mustard all over your tie.' Said Rizzuto, 'You huckleberry, that's not mustard—that's New Jersey!'"

—USA Today, August 1985

A Budding Ball Player

To say that Phil Rizzuto's rise to the top of the baseball world was simple and glorious is quite far from the truth. His story begins in the Ridgewood section of Brooklyn, an ethnically mixed community based just inside the Queens-Brooklyn border, back in 1917. Philip Francis Rizzuto was born to Philip Sr., and the former Rose Angotti on September 25, 1917, not 1918, as many publications and baseball cards indicate. The family had just moved to their new house on Dill Place, a tiny street that featured a handful of small homes. His two sisters, Mary and Rose, were born first and second, respectively. Phil's brother Alfred would follow in 1920.

Philip Sr., and Rose grew up in the downtown section of Brooklyn, near the Brooklyn Bridge, and several miles away from the Ridgewood section. It was there that they met and courted, and in 1913 they were married. Philip had been a laborer for the first few years of their marriage, and in early 1917, took a job as a trolley car conductor with the Brooklyn Rapid Transit Company. His route took him from Brooklyn to Queens and from Ridgewood to Richmond Hill. Later on, when Phil Jr., was old enough, he enjoyed meeting up with his father's car and giving him his lunch. In his new vocation, he was making more money, although not much more, than he had as a laborer. At least it was steady employment and as such, gave the family the opportunity to move into bigger quarters.

Like most kids growing up in New York, he got his induction into the world of baseball early on. When he was four years old, his father gave him a bat and glove. When he was eight, his mother graced him with a baseball uniform she had made. Phil loved baseball even then. He played whenever he could, no matter what the season. If it wasn't baseball, it was softball or stickball. When he wasn't playing baseball, or football—his speed made him a natural to run with the ball—Phil was attending PS 68. School aside, and church on Sunday, Phil played sports seven days a week, from daybreak to sundown. PS 68 did not have organized sports teams, but that didn't stop the local kids from finding a place to play baseball, which even then was Phil's favorite sport. Football to Phil was nothing more than a filler until there were enough guys to field two baseball teams. And so, like the others, Rizzuto would find a game somewhere, at a sandlot or in the streets.

Things were going fairly well for the Rizzutos, according to Joe Trimble in his book, *Phil Rizzuto*, which was released after the Scooter won the Most Valuable Player award in 1950 as part of the "Most Valuable Player Series" (its print run was short; the few copies in existence today are considered collectors' items). In fact, the whole country was enjoying good times in the 1920s. Philip Sr., figured it was a good time to switch jobs. He left his secure $40-a-week position with the transit and moved to a construction job that promised better money and a fine future. The money, indeed, was better and the work, it seemed, was endless. Here was a chance, he thought, to finally get his family over the hump, a chance to taste the better life, not to have to worry about living from paycheck to paycheck.

And for a while, it was great. Just before the crash of 1929, Philip was able to put away enough money so that the family could move to a new, bigger house in Glendale, Queens. It was a two-family unit made of stucco, with the Rizzutos living downstairs, while they rented the upstairs apartment. Phil, now 12, and his nine-year-old brother Alfred, shared a spacious basement, which included a pool table.

But as the times hit the country hard, so did they hit the Rizzutos. Philip lost his job building houses, and he was forced to go back to the transit and ask for his job back. However, since he had lost his 10-year seniority when he left the trolley company, he had to start all over again at the bottom. The work was sporadic, with Rizzuto becoming a part-time worker, filling in as needed. Like many other Americans at the time, the Rizzutos accepted home relief from the government to supplement their meager income. Rose, a whiz at sewing, now needed to perform her expertise for income. Phil, too, helped out, taking on a newspaper route in the neighborhood. Although he was not pressured to do so, his parents were thrilled that their son wanted to chip in with the family's finances. Furthermore, they didn't want his childhood overwhelmed by the rough times, and were glad to see him involved in the usual boyhood activities. In Phil's case, baseball.

By that time, young Phil—on the verge of becoming a teenager—had proven he could play ball with the best of them, and then some. He was an outfielder then, playing against boys much older than he. Phil played "in the streets, then in whatever leagues I could get into," Rizzuto told Leo Trachtenberg of *Yankees Magazine* many years later. "They had the Standard Union League, the Brooklyn Eagle League—I got more experience playing on those bad fields with rocks all over the infield."

One of the teams that the 12-year-old Rizzuto played on was called the Ridgewood Robins, named after the Brooklyn Robins, as the Dodgers were referred to because of their manager, Wilbert "Uncle Robbie" Robinson. Playing for this team was a feather in one's cap since everybody in Glendale was a Dodgers fan. The Rizzuto home was no different. Yet, tiny Phil nearly didn't make the team because of his size —he was razzed by the other kids — but he surprised both the team's coach, a Mr. Willenbuch, and his teammates, and made the club.

The team participated in a sandlot tournament sponsored by a Brooklyn newspaper, the *Standard Union*. The Robins played superbly and moved into the championship round, which was scheduled for Ebbets Field, home of the major league Robins. This in itself was a dream come true for Rizzuto and his family, faithful followers of the Brooklyn squad. The Robins knocked off the Coney Island Athletics for the title. For young Rizzuto, it was a great day even if he didn't get a hit.

"I was about four feet high then and was playing left field," he told Arthur Patterson years later. "Mr. Willenbuch wouldn't let me swing at all. First I'd bat left-handed, then right-handed, but I wasn't allowed to swing. I walked the first four times up, but on the fifth time the pitcher got two strikes on me so I had to swing. I fouled the ball and I was so low down that it rose up and hit the umpire right in the Adam's apple. Boy, was he sore."

In 1931, Phil enrolled at distant Richmond Hill High School, miles from his home but closer than any other high school. It was a trolley car ride away, and luckily for Phil, it was along his father's route. When the timing worked out, he was able to pocket the nickel fare and catch a ride on his father's car for free.

He did not have instant success there as a ballplayer. In fact, the 4-foot-11 Rizzuto did not go out for the team his first year there. He was going to, but a good friend of his was academically ineligible to play. Not knowing anybody on the team and being shy, Phil was reluctant to sign up. Back in his neighborhood, Rizzuto knew all the kids, even if many of them were older. He didn't bat an eye when they kidded him about his size, but the prospect of being hassled by guys he didn't know wasn't appealing to him. So instead of playing for Richmond Hill, he continued to ply his trade on the sandlots.

By the spring of 1933, though, Rizzuto was ready to roam the outfield for the high school team. But when Phil first met his coach, Al Kunitz, he was told that the outfield was out because of his size. Kunitz didn't think he could properly cover such a large area. Kunitz watched Rizzuto carefully during the tryouts, and although unsure about Rizzuto because of his size, Kunitz liked what he saw and pegged the kid for third base. Among his teammates that year was a nifty shortstop named Ralph Benzenberg, the team's captain, and second baseman Jimmy Castrataro. Benzenberg, the star of the team, would later sign a minor league contract with the Giants. Rather than remain in the bushes, he eventually got married and settled into a more consistent lifestyle.

By the end of that first season, Kunitz was convinced that Rizzuto had the talent to make it all the way, even if he was small. Kunitz was greatly impressed with Rizzuto's speed, heads-up play, and knack for the game. Rizzuto always seemed to know what he was doing out there. Kunitz, a former catcher for Columbia University and in the minor leagues, began working diligently with his protege and got word out to his baseball connections that he had something special here.

"He got me to practice the bunt, waiting to the last second and not tipping it off like a lot of these kids do today," Rizzuto remembered in *Yankees Magazine*. "He also taught me to steal bases, and everything a little guy could do."

Kunitz played another important role in the baseball life of Rizzuto. In an effort to calm down the youngster after a bad call one day, he warned Phil not to lose his cool on the field, that it could cost his team a victory.

Rizzuto recalled in a *USA Today* story, "Mr. Al Kunitz, he asked me, 'What expression do you use when you get excited?' Ever since I was a kid, I would say, 'Holy cow!' Or, 'You huckleberry!' So, that's what I'd say, and it was great advice. I never got thrown out." To this day, he is known to thousands of baseball fans all around the world for these colorful expressions.

On the field, Rizzuto continued to excel. He was Richmond Hills's captain in 1934 and responded with a .354 batting average. The *Long Island Press*, a Queens daily newspaper, called

Rizzuto the best third baseman in the city. By now, Kunitz was absolutely sure that Rizzuto could make it big. A few years earlier, he spotted another major league prospect under him, Marius Russo, a left-handed pitcher who hurled for Kunitz. Russo went on to pitch for Long Island University and later the Yankees (Rizzuto and Russo were Yankee teammates for the 1941 and 1942 seasons).

"He gave me the idea that I could become a professional ball player, and that gave me quite a kick," Rizzuto said in a 1951 *Sporting News* interview. "Kunitz kept asking scouts to watch me, but I had no professional notions. Al kept saying, 'Sure, you are small. But you will fill out. You are fast, a great fielder, you have acute baseball sense.' I shook my head in affirmation and laughed."

Kunitz explained to Phil that he needed all the experience he could garner. As a result, Phil played every weekend during the summer months for the Glendale Browns of the Queens Alliance League. In 1935 he joined a semi-pro team from Floral Park, way out on Long Island, where he made $120 for an 80-game season. Rizzuto beat out several quality players at short-stop, proving during tryouts that he was the best candidate for the important position. However, you won't see Rizzuto's name in any of the team's box scores. He did not go by the name of Rizzuto while playing for Floral Park. Scholastic rules forbid playing for money, so Phil used the last name of Reilly.

Playing for Floral Park was a great experience for Rizzuto. The squad took on a number of teams from the area, plus they entertained more sophisticated clubs like the Black Yankees. In fact, during his Floral Park days, Rizzuto batted against the great black pitcher, Satchel Paige, on more than one occasion.

In a recent TV interview, Rizzuto recalled hitting against Paige. "He was so fast," the Scooter said. "I remember one time I thought I had hit the ball so hard and I'm running to first and all of a sudden, there's Satchel going towards the first-base line. My bat had broke in half and the ball was tapped down the line. I beat it out because he was slow, but oh boy, was he fast (throwing)."

In the spring of 1935, Phil had another bang-up season for Richmond Hill. Benzenberg had graduated, opening the way for Rizzuto to move in at shortstop. He did an outstanding job, and *The Press* this time selected him as the top shortstop in the city. Scouts began visiting the Queens high school more regularly to catch a glimpse of Rizzuto.

"The first major scout to watch me represented the Cardinals," Rizzuto recalled in *The Sporting News*. "I got three hits that afternoon, played a whale of a game in the field. That was in June, 1935. I weighed 135.

"The ivory hunter from St. Louis deplored my lack of size. He said he was sorry he could not recommend me, but he did do me a big favor. He got me the job with the Floral Park semi-pros."

The Boston Red Sox came calling next. A scout reportedly made Rizzuto an offer calling for $250 a month. Just as quickly as he made the offer, however, the scout disappeared. Rizzuto, who was ready to jump at the deal, was left out in the cold. Kunitz rallied the youth, told him to keep hanging in there. With the pro scouts turned off by his size, though, Rizzuto considered college. It was not something he relished since he was not a big fan of school anyway, but it was a way to keep playing ball and keep his professional dream alive.

Both Columbia University and Fordham University showed an interest in the diminutive shortstop. Columbia seriously considered Rizzuto, but his grades were below acceptable standards. Fordham, however, liked Phil because they thought he could become a football player! With his speed, they thought he could elude defenses like the plague. Rizzuto considered that option, but in the end, nothing happened. Finally, Phil took a job with S. Gumpert & Co., manufacturers of foodstuffs for hotels.

Despite all these setbacks, Rizzuto was determined more than ever to play major league ball. It was only a matter of time, he figured, which was one of the main reasons he took the job with S. Gumpert & Co. Rizzuto was drawn to the company, in great part, because it also had a ball team. Until something better came along, like a major league offer, this would do.

With the realization that college ball was now out, Phil's interest in remaining in high school wavered. Finally, in the spring of 1936, he left Richmond Hill High School. Trimble, who was a top-notch reporter with the *New York Daily News*, wrote in the book, *Phil Rizzuto*, "Rizzuto was back in school in 1936 but, as the gag goes, he wasn't taking up anything but space. French and other languages were throwing him and he was playing hookey too often to keep up with his classmates.

"By mutual consent, Rizzuto and Richmond Hill severed their connection in the spring of that year. Any education which would benefit him in later life would have to come on the diamond." According to Trimble, "Rizzuto did get a diploma, gratis, many years later. In 1948 the school held its seventy-fifth anniversary celebration and all students who had gone on to success in life were awarded diplomas and certified as graduates." Rizzuto may have ended his association with Richmond Hill's educational process, but his relationship with Kunitz remained strong, as his former coach continued to pursue a baseball career for the talented youth.

In the summer of 1936, Rizzuto nearly struck out in his bid for the major leagues. He made three serious attempts during open tryouts that year, and failed in the first two, with the Dodgers and then the Giants. Actually, failed is not the right word. In truth, Rizzuto was not given much of a chance.

Contrary to most recent published accounts, Casey Stengel was not on hand when Rizzuto visited Ebbets Field for a tryout with the Dodgers. Instead, two Dodgers coaches—Otto Miller and Zach Taylor—conducted the morning tryout as they had many others, with anywhere from 150 to 300 16- to 18-year-old sandlotters hoping for a serious look.

"I had a good summer," Rizzuto said in *The Sporting News.* "I hit against Satchel Paige and other good pitchers. Then I was invited to Ebbets Field, where Casey Stengel was running the Dodgers. This was in 1936. The story is that Stengel chased me out of the park. It is not true. Casey never saw me." Ironically, Rizzuto himself has claimed in some accounts that Stengel was there for the tryout.

"It wasn't much of a tryout," Rizzuto recalled in a 1941 interview. "They'd line up about 300 of us on the left-field foul line and run us to the right-field wall. The slowest guys were dropped out. I got there in time, but nobody gave me a second look. Yes, I was the smallest man there, too. Everyone wonders about my size. I've had a great deal of trouble convincing people I am a ball player—even some managers."

In another interview, Rizzuto said, "The first 50 to finish (the race across the field) were told to stay, the rest were invited to go home. A simple system, it struck me. I was one of the early finishers, so I stayed."

Not for long, although long enough to get stung in the back with a pitched ball during batting practice. Unable to shake off the injury, Rizzuto could not muster a meaningful at-bat in his short stint in the batter's box.

"A big right-handed kid was pitching," Rizzuto remembered in Trimble's book. "I had been a good hitter in high school at Richmond Hill and even managed to get my base hits in semi-pro competition on Long Island. I was nervous but I felt sure I would at least hit the ball. But I never did get much chance to. The first pitch hit me squarely in the middle of the back and knocked me down. It hurt like the devil, and the wind was knocked out of me. I probably should have gotten out of the batter's box and rested until the pain left. But I didn't want them to think I was afraid. So I stepped right in again. Then I could hardly swing, and, after missing a couple of pitches, heard Miller say, 'Okay, sonny. That's all. I don't think you'll do little fellow. Good thing you didn't get hurt by that big guy.'"

"One of the Brooklyn coaches told me I was too small," Rizzuto noted in *The Sporting News*. "He told me to try something else, and forget baseball as a possible means for a livelihood."

About a month later, Rizzuto got a letter from the New York Giants regarding a tryout with them. Phil was sure that he'd get a fair shot this time. But this time, the visit was shorter than his Dodgers stay. Much shorter, and much more humiliating.

"My experience with the Giants was even briefer," Rizzuto continued in *The Sporting News* story. "A scout for the club asked me to come to the Polo Grounds. Pancho Snyder took one look at me, refused me a uniform and a tryout, and said, 'Kid, you are too frail for baseball. Stay and watch the Giants play the Reds, if you like, but we can't use you." To add insult to injury, Snyder supposedly told Rizzuto to "go home and get yourself a shoeshine box!"

Meanwhile, all along, Paul Krichell, renowned chief of the New York Yankee scouts, had been following the career of Rizzuto, unbeknownst to the kid from Queens. Alerted to Rizzuto by another scout, George Mack, Krichell had seen Rizzuto play on several occasions. But it wasn't until his failures with the Dodgers and Giants that Rizzuto heard from Krichell. "Krich," as he was called, was a catcher briefly for the St. Louis Browns. In two seasons (1911-1912), Krichell, whose height and weight practically mirrored Rizzuto's major league figures, batted .222. He played in just 85 games and never amounted to much at that level. Of his 54 hits, nine were doubles. He had no other extra-base hits, scored only 25 runs, and drove in a meager 16. Hardly major league numbers. As a scout, he more than made up for his lack of clout as a player. As the Yanks' chief scout, he had the final say in many of the great organization's signings. Krichell joined the Yankees as a scout in 1920 and had a big hand in putting together that outstanding 1927 Yankee team, signing Gehrig, Tony Lazzeri, and Mark Koenig.

In August, Krichell sent Phil an invitation to a tryout at Yankee Stadium. Confident on one hand, fearful on the other, Rizzuto was hesitant to go, but did so after consulting with his family. Phil's greatest fear was that another swarm of kids would cover the field and he would get lost in the shuffle. Imagine his amazement when he got there that morning and only a couple of dozen players were on the field for warm-ups. As soon as the shock wore off, Rizzuto was ecstatic. He knew he had a real chance this time.

Rizzuto recalled the Yankees' letter and subsequent events in an interview with Dan Daniel, writing for *The Sporting News*. "Next came an invitation from the Yankees," Rizzuto said. "By this time I was fed up with the 'too small, too frail' routine. But I went to the stadium, and there I met Paul Krichell, the first man from a major league club to give me any encouragement. They picked two teams and I was on one of the nines. That was progress. We played four or five innings every day. I started at second, shifted to third, and then was placed at short. I remember I hit a couple into the seats."

It was a wonderful week for Rizzuto. Not only did he feel as if he was getting a real chance to show his stuff, but he got to see Yankee greats like Lou Gehrig, Bill Dickey, Joe DiMaggio, and Tony Lazzeri warming up before games (the Yankees only played day games at the time). Krichell oversaw the Yankees wanna-bes games, along with Yankee coach Art Fletcher. Within a couple of days, Krichell and Fletcher agreed that Rizzuto had talent and made the kid an offer to join the Yankees' Class-D Pennsylvania State League club.

Rizzuto continued, "Krichell said to me, 'Rizzuto, I think you might have it. Would you care to go away?' I said that I had a job, but might become interested in a baseball career. So they sent me a contract with the Butler, Pennsylvania, club, $75 a month. I kicked. I was getting $18 a week, and living at home. I was working in a factory making hotel supplies, and played on their team in a Twilight League on the Prospect Park Parade Grounds. I had hit .430 in that league. I told Krichell that $75 was too little to live on. He sent me another contract and explained that in the Bi-State League I would have a longer season (because of the milder weather the season started a month earlier), giving me an extra $75." Rizzuto also stated, "I thought that was pretty good money. The kids around home who had jobs were making $12 a week then."

Another tale in *Yankees Magazine*, had Rizzuto discussing the minor league contract with Yankee general manager Ed Barrow. "We'd like to sign you to a minor league contract," Barrow reportedly said to Rizzuto. "Where and how much?" countered Phil. "Butler, Pennsylvania, at $70 a month." "Gee, I'd like to make a little more than that," answered Rizzuto. Barrow counter-offered, "We'll give you $75 a month and send you to Bassett, Virginia. That's it. Sign or get out of here."

In reality, Barrow would never have gotten involved with a minor league deal. Barrow did say years later that "Rizzuto cost me fifteen cents, ten for postage and five for a cup of coffee we gave him the last day he worked out at the Stadium."

Interestingly, Rizzuto was not the only future professional baseball player in the crowd that week. Tommy Holmes and Jim Prendergast would later play in the National League, Holmes with the Braves, Prendergast with the Cardinals and Phillies. Ironically, though, only Rizzuto was deemed good enough for a contract that tryout.

Rizzuto quickly decided that the offer to join the Class-D Bassett team was a good one and the next day brought his mother to the Bronx to sign the contract for him since he was a minor. A few months later, Phil Rizzuto stepped onto the Bassett field as a professional baseball player. A major league career was about to take off.

"He really tricked me into doing it. [Rock singer] Meat Loaf is a big Yankee fan. He's at the Stadium whenever he's not in concert. He said, 'I've got an idea for a song and I want you to do this bit of play-by-play. I haven't written the other lyrics yet, but this will go between the lyrics.' I had no idea, so I went up to do it.

"He gave me this thing to read and I kept saying, 'Why is every play a close play? And why, at the end, when the guy is coming home, do I have to say, Holy Cow! and then have to stop?' He says, 'Don't worry.'

"About eight months later my son came home with the album, and this song was called 'Paradise by the Dashboard Light.' My son thought I was a big rock star. He played it for me and I had to listen six or seven times to get the idea of what was going on. And when I realized what it was—about this kid trying to score—oh, jeez!

"The publicity was unbelievable. I was getting calls from stations for interviews, and Meat Loaf wanted me to go on tour with him. But the ones who got me, of course, were priests, teachers and parents."

—*Phil Rizzuto, rock star, Inside Sports*

2

A Minor League Star

Phil Rizzuto Sr., concerned that thieves could be on the train to Bassett, Virginia, pinned $20 to his son's undershirt on that spring day in 1937. Rizzuto Sr. was not sold on this idea of a baseball career for his son. He saw baseball only as a kids' game, not as a way to make a living. He let his son know it, too. "I'll let you try this," he said. "But if you don't make it right away, then you have to go out and find work." His mother wasn't so sure about this baseball thing, either, although she organized a party for family and friends before he departed for his first ever trip out of New York.

"I wasn't so sure that it was the best thing," Rizzuto's mother said in Joe Trimble's book. "He was so small and he didn't look very much like a ball player. Even though Mr. Krichell had assured me he would be all right, I was not very happy. His dad and I both felt that the Yankees were too big a team and that he was too little to make the major leagues. This going to Bassett, a place we had never heard of, didn't seem like the best thing for him. I wished it had been somewhere closer to home."

Phil didn't run into thieves as his father feared, and soon arrived in Bassett, a few miles from the North Carolina border and about 40 miles south of Roanoke. The town, named after E. D. Bassett, who owned a huge furniture factory and employed many of the 3,500 people living there, was your typical southern town, complete with Jim Crow-type laws affecting the 1,000 or so blacks living there.

Rizzuto, like the other ball players, lived in a boarding house in town. It was not an easy life, though, with the team seemingly always on the run. There were very few multiple-game series, with the club hopping back and forth among the Bi-State League's eight cities located within the borders of Virginia and North Carolina.

"We never stayed overnight in another town," Rizzuto told Trimble. "It was back on the bus after every game. We never saw a hotel at all. Each of us got 35 cents a day meal money. The league rules set a limit of 15 players on each squad. We had two catchers, six pitchers, and the seven other players. If anyone was hurt or a pinch-hitter was needed, a pitcher had to go into the game in some other position, as an outfielder or infielder."

Things were going well for the hopeful youngster out of Queens. Two weeks into the season, the little guy was getting a lot of attention for his play on the field and at the bat as Bassett held down first place. Rizzuto was getting into a fine groove when his budding career suddenly took a turn for the worse.

"I was running to first one day and stepped into a gopher hole," Rizzuto told Jim Ogle, writing for *Yankees Magazine*. "I heard something pop (in my left leg) and it really hurt. We didn't have trainers or anything in D ball in those days. Ray White, an old teammate on the sandlots, was the manager and also the trainer, bus driver and road secretary. Every night he would rub my leg, but it kept getting worse."

The pain was agonizing, yet Rizzuto continued to play in the days ahead. Finally, in mid-May, an old-time umpire working a game only because he lived in town, warned Rizzuto. "An old umpire took me aside one day and said, 'Look kid, you are badly hurt, and the sooner you get to a hospital, the better.'" He told Rizzuto that he'd seen legs like that before and it wasn't a problem that was going to go away by itself.

There was no doctor in Bassett so, as Rizzuto recalled in *The Sporting News*, "We were near Roanoke, Virginia. I went to a hospital there and saw a Dr. Johnson. He said, 'Young man, you have a muscle so badly pulled apart that gangrene has set in. About a week more and you would lose your leg. You will have to have an immediate operation.'" Since Rizzuto was underage, the doctor needed permission to perform the surgery. Rose Rizzuto wanted to be there for the operation, but the doctor insisted that he could not wait, since the gangrene had set in. While Rose, an uncle, and Phil's brother Alfred were taking the train to Roanoke, Phil underwent surgery.

"When I woke up 17 hours later," he told Ogle, "my mother, uncle, and brother were around my bed and the doctor told me I would never play again. In fact, for a bit, they thought of amputation. The doctor cut six inches off the muscle and tied the ends to other muscles. I have a big hole in my leg and it extends from my knee to the thigh, but I fooled the doctor." And his mother, as well. Rose saw the 37 stitches and knew of the hole and told her son that his baseball career was over, that he should come home and consider another occupation. Actually, Phil was pretty devastated at the time, too, and wondered quietly about his future as he exercised the leg as best he could while recovering in Bassett.

"I was out of action for three months," he told *The Sporting News*. "When I came back I was afraid my career had ended. I had been quite a runner. In high school I used to steal second and third.

"The doctor said, 'Walk a week. Then go out and run as hard as you can. In a minute you will know if you are finished or will be able to continue with your career.'" Rizzuto followed the doctor's directions, walked for a week, then prepared for his day of reckoning. Rizzuto got to the ballpark, took a deep breath, and ran as hard as he could. "I cut loose and the muscle held," he remembers. And not only did the muscle hold, but so did Little

Phil's ability to play ball. He ended up playing 67 games, batting .310, with 53 runs scored, 17 doubles, five triples, five home runs, 32 RBIs, and six stolen bases to help Bassett win the Bi-State League pennant.

The next season, Rizzuto was rewarded for his outstanding play by being promoted to Class B Norfolk of the Piedmont League, his salary doubling to $150 per month. Norfolk, Virginia, by the Chesapeake Bay and a short spin from Newport News and Virginia Beach, enjoyed a full year of Rizzuto, who was joined by his manager at Bassett, Ray White. There were several future major leaguers on the club, from Billy Johnson to Aaron Robinson to Gerry Priddy to Rizzuto.

As for Phil, he started slowly, with incumbent and popular shortstop Claude Corbitt ripping the hide off the ball. Before long Corbitt was shipped to Single-A Augusta (Georgia), to tougher pitching, opening the door for Rizzuto. With his competition out of the picture, Rizzuto turned it on early in the season at High Rock Park and never let up, hitting .336, with 97 runs scored, 24 doubles, 10 triples, nine homers, 58 RBIs, and 26 stolen bases. Corbitt, who eventually played briefly in the major leagues (as a weak-hitting reserve with Brooklyn and Cincinnati), had a decent season at Augusta, but quickly went down the totem pole with the Yankee brass. Rizzuto, meanwhile, had become a crowd favorite with the Norfolk fans, making them forget about Corbitt. The press took a liking to Phil, as well, and began referring to him as "The Flea," in reference to his speed and size.

The 1938 season also marked the first of a three-year working relationship between Rizzuto and second baseman Priddy. In the years to follow, they would become the talk of the minor leagues. At Norfolk they became an awesome double play combination, and off the field they were great buddies. Priddy, who was from California, could pound the ball. He hit .323 in 1938, socked six triples, nine home runs, and slugged 36 doubles, most in the circuit.

At the end of the year, another pennant winner for

Rizzuto, the New Yorker was edged out by Charlotte's Roberto Estalella, by one vote, as the league's MVP. The Cuban-born Estalella, who had a couple of cups of coffee with the Washington Senators prior to 1938, never amounted to much in the major leagues in a career that moved him from Washington to the St. Louis Browns, back to Washington, and then to the Philadelphia Athletics. Estalella was one of those veteran players who benefited from World War II. Primarily an outfielder, he was pretty much a regular from 1942 to 1945, then dropped out of sight once the war ended. Rizzuto, who would miss three years because of World War II, was still three years away from the big time, but with two seasons under his belt, was making a name for himself.

"In 1939 I was promoted all the way to Kansas City," Rizzuto noted in *The Sporting News*. "I will never forget that spring training season. The older players made life miserable for me. They played every conceivable trick on me. Buzz Boyle's idea of comedy was to get hold of a letter from your family, tear it to bits, and lay them neatly on the bench near you."

"I think (pitcher) Johnny Lindell was the No. 1 prankster," says Sid Bordman, who joined the Blues organization in 1940 as the batboy. "He picked on him (Rizzuto) a lot. He was the ringleader. They used to nail his shorts to a locker and do all sorts of stuff like that. They picked on him a lot in Kansas City."

"Oh man, I remember a lot of things about Little Phil," recalls Billy Hitchcock. "He's just a great guy, a wonderful little fella. We always teased him. He's very naive, you know, and he was always the butt of all the jokes fellas would pull on him. He'd go along with them and I always said, that Rizzuto, he's dumb like a fox. He knew what was going on all that time, but he allowed everybody to have a good time and get a lot of fun out of it. He'd just go along with it. He was a grand fella, very good-hearted, very personable, very likeable. He was just a youngster then, of course, but he was a fine fella and what a ball player."

Bill Meyer, the Kansas City Blues manager and future skipper of the Pittsburgh Pirates, wasn't sure initially where to use Rizzuto, who was now earning $300 a month. Hitchcock, an outstanding athlete who had played football at Auburn University, was a candidate for the shortstop position, as was Rizzuto. Jack Saltzgaver, who had been a Yankee reserve for several years, was pegged as the third baseman, with Gerry Priddy at second base. Hitchcock, who missed the 1938 season because of a knee injury, had a terrific spring training, making Meyer's decision that much more difficult. In the end, the manager decided to go with Rizzuto at short, in great part because he wasn't sure how Hitchcock would perform on a day-to-day basis after the year layoff because of the knee.

"I ran into tough competition for the shortstop job from Billy Hitchcock," Rizzuto told *The Sporting News*. "He had a real big spring. I rarely look good during spring training. It looked like Hitchcock at short, with Jack Saltzgaver at third. I got a break. Hitchcock had a bad knee, a souvenir from his football days at Auburn. The knee bothered him so I got the job."

"I had played shortstop at college," says Hitchcock, who eventually moved to third base, replacing Saltzgaver. "I reported to Kansas City in the spring of 1939. I don't think they expected me to play at Kansas City because that was my first year. Jack Saltzgaver was there. He was the third baseman. Phil and Gerry, of course, had been playing at Norfolk and they figured that would be the double play combination. I don't know, I just had a good spring and things went well for me down there. Bill Meyer decided to take me north as a utility infielder and as it turned out, Saltzgaver couldn't play every day, and I started to play a lot of third base that year."

Rizzuto got the full-time shortstop job in 1939, when, he said, he "first saw *pitching*," and responded in scintillating fashion. By mid-season he was recognized as one of the league's best players, prompting a press release from the American Association, dated for release June 29, 1939:

"Newcomers Worth Watching in the American Association"

Phil Rizzuto, Kansas City

Good things, it has been said, come in small packages. Officials of the Kansas City Blues are willing to attest to the truth of this statement every time they look at or think of one Philip F. Rizzuto, a young man who has been playing a lot of baseball for the Blues around the shortfield ever since the season opened.

As far as size is concerned, Mr. Rizzuto might be termed one of the "runts" of the American Association, but when it comes to playing ability that is quite a different story. The youngster, who won't reach his majority until September 25, is only 5 ft. 6 in. tall and weighs a mere 155 pounds, but he packs plenty of wallop in the Louisville Slugger that he totes to the plate with him several times daily.

When Rizzuto arrived at the Blues spring training base in Haines City, Florida, last March, the experts gave him the once over a couple of times and then decided that while he might have some natural talent he was too small to do much good in the American Association with its speedy style of play.

But the Glendale, N.Y., boy quickly made those who had shaken their heads "eat dem woids," for the training season wasn't many days old before he was one of the sensations of the camp. Even then the Blues followers weren't overly optimistic. "Wait," they said, "until the pitchers start curving 'em and we'll see what happens."

The pitchers did and they did. In other words, it made little difference to young Philip what kind of pitchers were tossed in his general direction for they usually went back faster then they came up.

Opening day came and Rizzuto was in the lineup at short-stop. It might be recorded that he's still in there and, barring injury, there doesn't seem a chance in the world for anyone to get him out of there.

This is only his third year in professional ball and a great future is predicted for him. He's hit over .300 each year. He has shown he's a natural hitter. It doesn't seem to make a great deal of difference to him whether he is facing Class D pitching at Bassett, the Class B hurling at Norfolk, or the Class AA chucking at Kansas City. They all appear to look alike to Philip.

xxx

Rizzuto again was on a pennant winner, his third straight in professional ball. Kansas City, aided by Vince DiMaggio's league-leading 46 homers, took the American Association flag in a breeze as it won 107 games. Rizzuto did his part, batting .316, with 99 runs scored, 21 doubles, six triples, five home runs, 64 RBIs, and a career-high fielding percentage of .944. So did the 6-foot Priddy, who batted .333, cracked a league-leading 44 doubles, hit 15 triples, 24 home runs, and drove in 107 runs. Meyer earned *The Sporting News's* Minor League Manager of the Year award for his efforts.

It was during that 1939 season that Rizzuto gained his now famous nickname, "Scooter." There is some confusion as to who actually tagged the nickname on Rizzuto, but most evidence points toward Hitchcock. For years, Rizzuto himself attributed the "name caller" as Hitchcock. Others — including Bordman — say it was the veteran, Ralph "Buzz" Boyle, who gave him the moniker.

"Billy Hitchcock was from a little southern town and they have these quaint expressions," Rizzuto told *Inside Sports* magazine. "I had little legs and short, quick steps. He'd say, 'Man, you're not running, you're scooting.'"

"I really and truly thought I was the one who called him Scooter," insists Hitchcock. "Anybody'd ask why, well, one of the most greatest and exciting things is to watch Rizzuto hit a triple. He was a little short fella, you know, and he'd take these short little strides, but he could run and he'd hit a triple. When he'd round first base and go into second base it always seemed as he rounded second that he'd lose his cap. He had a pretty good nose and he had that curly hair and he'd round second and lose his cap and here he'd go scooting around the bases and just slide into third base head first in a cloud of dust. I'd say he looked like a scooter running around the infield. This is my thought on the thing, and I think I was the one who put the 'Scooter' on him."

In 1940, even without DiMaggio's 46 homers (he moved on to Cincinnati and then Pittsburgh), Kansas City was a power-house and won the pennant again. For Phil, it was four pennants in four seasons. The Blues had an infield that many people felt was the greatest minor league infield ever assembled, with Hitchcock at third, Rizzuto at short, Priddy at second, and Johnny Sturm at first. Rizzuto and Priddy were the featured attractions, of course. Reportedly after the 1938 season, Yankee general manager Ed Barrow was offered $250,000 for the two.

"Those two teams (1939-40) were great teams," says Bordman, who was with the organization for several years, beginning in 1940 as a 16-year-old bat boy. "That infield was intact for two years, probably the greatest minor league infield of all time. Probably better than a lot of major league infields." Rizzuto, Priddy, and Sturm were all promoted to the Yankees in 1941, while Hitchcock was sold to Detroit at the end of the 1941 Blues campaign.

"At the end of the '41 season the Yankees sold me to Detroit," remembers Hitchcock. "At the time, Newark (the Newark Bears, the Yankees' Triple A club on the east coast) had a real good ballclub and we had a good ballclub. The Yankees just had a lot of good, young players and up to that time, pretty much held on to them. Things began to change. They began to trade and sell ball players and that's what gave me my opportunity to play with Detroit. I couldn't play short or third with Rizzuto, and of course Red Rolfe was playing third base at the time. I was sort of extra baggage, I guess, so that's the reason they sold me. It was a break for me."

Realizing the marketability of Rizzuto early in the 1940 season, the American Association was prompted to distribute a press release, partly tongue-in-cheek, on April 30 regarding the spunky shortstop from Kansas City:

Baseball players have been known to admit to hobbies of every kind and variety, but it remains for one Philip Francis Rizzuto, Kansas City's $100,000 shortstop to come up with one of the most unique.

In filling out his questionnaire for the league's press and radio bureau, the sensational young shortfielder of the American Association champions confesses that his favorite hobby is— believe it or not— snipe hunting.

And from all reports of his teammates, young Philip is developing into a snipe hunter of the first order. It seems that he has already made several extended journeys in quest of the elusive snipe but reports as to the success of his ventures vary. In any event, Rizzuto has never yet turned down an invitation for such a foray and thus is entitled to any honors that may be available for this type of sporting activity. Questioned as to the number of snipes he has "bagged" in his numerous expeditions, Rizzuto merely grinned and replied somewhat phlegmatically, "I ain't a sayin'."

Phil is equally frank in the remainder of his questionnaire. In answer to the question as to his nationality he replies bluntly, "Dago." As for his plans when his baseball days are over he tells them in three words— "raise a family." At the moment, however, Philip is quite unencumbered by a wife.

His biggest thrill in baseball came on the day when his team made six double plays to tie a league record, while outside of the national game, sensation number one was in meeting some movie stars in New York.

Rizzuto is quite a movie and radio fan. His favorite actor is Mickey Rooney while Lana Turner is the number one actress. He liked "Gone With the Wind" better than any other picture he has seen in the last year while he placed "Earl of Chicago" at the bottom of the list.

In radio, Bob Hope and Judy Garland are his favorites while the Kay Kyser and Jack Benny programs are "tops" with him. His favorite news commentator is Walter Winchell, while Walt Lochman, Kansas City baseball broadcaster, leads the parade of the nation's sports announcers by a country mile, according to the Blues' young infield star.

Joe DiMaggio is his favorite ball player of the present day, while of those not now active, "Babe" Ruth is his idol.

Rizzuto is a resident of Glendale, Long Island, New York, where he was born 21 years ago last September 25. Only 5 ft. 6 in. tall, and weighing but 155 pounds, he nevertheless packs a lusty wallop in his war club. He bats and throws right-handed.

This is his fourth year in the minors—and if the "wise ones" are right, his last one. He started his career with Bassett, Virginia, of the Bi-State League in 1937, advancing to Norfolk, Virginia, of the Piedmont for the 1938 campaign.

Last year he was one of the key players of Kansas City's great championship club and he gives promise of being an even greater player now that he has one year of AA baseball experience under his belt. Unless all the experts are wrong, he's destined to become a great major league star.

Rizzuto's off-seasons are spent in his native Glendale, where, for recreation he does a lot of bowling. He works as a baker when not playing ball. In other words, during the summer he makes the dough and during the winter he kneads it.

xxx

Rizzuto ended up having his best minor league season in 1940, batting a career-high .347 with 124 runs scored, 28 doubles, 10 triples, 10 home runs, 73 RBIs, and 35 stolen bases. As a baserunner, he had so many jittery moves that opposing pitchers were easily riled, many believing his gyrations were actually signals to hitters as to the next pitch. Future major leaguer hurler Johnny VanderMeer, for one, threatened to hit Rizzuto in the head if he didn't stop "stealing signs." During that terrific season, when it all came together for Rizzuto, he had a fielding percentage of .949 that included a record-breaking number of double plays. Rizzuto was in on 130 of the team's 194 double plays, most of which involved Priddy. In addition, he led the American Association in assists and putouts at shortstop.

He was named the league's all-star shortstop for the fourth consecutive year and was named the American Association Most Valuable Player. Rizzuto was the first choice of six of the eight members of the voting committee (American Association media) and was second on a seventh ballot. One voter did not place Rizzuto's name on the ballot. Rizzuto garnered 55 points while Minneapolis outfielder Ab Wright was second with 42, after leading the league in hitting. Walker Cooper (who got one first-place vote), a catcher with Columbus, was third with 27 points. Outfielder Chet Morgan of Louisville was fourth in the voting, and pitcher Bob Logan of Indianapolis was fifth. Rizzuto's double play partner, Gerry Priddy, got one first-place vote, but gained just eight overall points. Priddy finished the year with an average of .306 and 112 runs batted in.

In the months ahead, *The Sporting News* panel of sports writers voted Rizzuto the outstanding player in all of minor league baseball for 1940. With nothing more to prove in the minors, Rizzuto would soon be summoned to Yankee Stadium.

"I made the trip to the Yankee offices to sign my first contract before going south in 1941, and was ushered into (general manager Ed) Barrow's office. I did not know Barrow. I did not know that the man in the frayed sweater, being shaved by a guy whom he kept calling Goulash, was Barrow. I sat silent until Goulash finished. Then the gent who had just been shaved sat up and looked at me hard from under his beetling eyebrows. 'Young man, what is your trouble?' I told him I wanted more money. He shouted, 'I give you this and no more. If okay, sign. If not, get the hell out of here.' I signed."

—*Phil Rizzuto, The Sporting News*

3

Welcome to the Big Time

They came as a package, Phil Rizzuto and Gerry Priddy. Together since Norfolk, the two had become synonymous with "keystone combination" —and winning. Like Rizzuto, Priddy had played on four straight championship clubs. At Kansas City, they were the greatest minor league double play combination ever, or so they said. Now, they were heading for New York City, the both of them.

"I have played alongside Gerry Priddy for three years, and it would be great to continue with him on the Yankees," Rizzuto told Dan Daniel writing for the *The World-Telegram* at the St. Petersburg training camp in late February 1941. "He is the best second sacker I have seen. He can get rid of the ball from any position, has an easy-motion throw across the body that is made for double plays, he's shifty, has baseball instinct, he's fast and dashes into the outfield for relays. As a hitter, he has plenty of power to right and left center. As you know, like me, he bats right-handed."

Arthur E. Patterson of the *New York Herald Tribune* pointed out, "Rizzuto and Priddy have worked on a lot of signals and tricks around second base. At least seven times during the last two seasons with the Blues they have made one-out 'double plays.' In other words they have both gone after balls hit right over second and, when unable to make the throw to first, have flipped the ball to the other for a relay out."

"You get used to working with the same fellow" Rizzuto said simply.

Daniel described the pair this way in another article:

"Gerry Priddy, who is sandy-haired and pale-faced, is the exact opposite of the lad with whom he is moving into a fourth straight season around second. The Californian is quiet. Rarely does he break into a smile. Seldom does he say anything. Not lacking in ideas, but naturally reticent. Priddy is not as fleet of foot as Rizzuto. Nor does Gerry look to be as good a hitter. He, too, is right-handed, and his power also lies in left field. However, he can drive home runs into right field seats, and down South he cleared a centerfield fence that was 388 feet from the plate.

"Rizzuto may poke an occasional homer. But he is not a four-base hitter. Priddy is. He likes the ball rather high. As a second sacker, Gerry makes a perfect team with Phil. Both get the ball away with remarkable speed. In fact, they may have to slow down the getaway just a trifle to put more on the ball. Phil and Gerry are the first pair to come into the American League after long experience as an infield combination since Joe Boley and Max Bishop hopped from the Orioles to the Athletics in 1924."

Former Kansas City bat boy and later a sportswriter for the *Kansas City Star*, Sid Bordman recalls that Rizzuto and Priddy "were good friends and a great double play combination, but really, they were different type people. Priddy was sort of a hot dog in a way. Thought he was pretty darn good, and he was. But Rizzuto was never like that. He never had a big head."

During the winter of 1940-41, the two kept in contact, sending clippings to each other, keeping each other abreast of any developments involving them. There were some trade rumors (the Detroit Tigers, in particular, were very interested in either of the two), almost always involving Priddy, and the two discussed their merit.

Once the 1940 season was over, it was quite clear that both Rizzuto and Priddy were expected to make the Yankees in 1941. Both, of course, were coming off excellent seasons. However, another reason for both infielders coming up at the time, was that Commissioner Kenesaw Landis was beginning to make waves about the farm system, in particular those run by the Yankees and Dodgers, which he saw as unfair to many of the ball clubs. The Yankees, who controlled a great number of minor league teams and players, did not want to hasten any decision by Landis, who had proven many times in the past that he wasn't going to be pushed around. The last thing the Yankee brass wanted to do was to push Landis's button and have him do something to spoil its outstanding minor league system. And so, while Rizzuto was a sure thing for 1941, Priddy was in a way, expendable. After all, 26-year-old Joe Gordon was doing a great job already at second base. There was no rush to bring up another second baseman.

As early as the summer of 1940, sportswriter Joe Williams wrote that "The way things stand now the Yankees aren't going to be able to make room for both boys. How could Priddy, good as they say he is, ever hope to get Joe Gordon off second base, for example? Rizzuto, it would seem, has a better chance to make the team, because Frank Crosetti, the shortstop, is getting along. One of these days, he will have to be replaced."

It was Williams's vision that Rizzuto would make the Yankees and that Priddy would be sold to another ball club. He went on to say, "This will come close to breaking up the hearts of the youngsters. They are inseparable. They have a juvenile notion they must be teamed up to play good baseball. They want to come to the big leagues together. That's all they talk about. Naturally they'd rather come to the Yankees than any other club. But apparently that's out. After this season, the greatest double play combination the minors ever saw seems definitely fated to be broken up."

Williams did not come up with these revelations by himself. It was Ed Barrow, president of the Yankees, who told him, "It's going to be a crime to break up that combination. But it's one of those things we'll just have to do." The closer 1941 approached, though, the more it seemed as if both were headed for New York. Priddy had performed well enough that the Yankees did not want to lose him, and McCarthy was apparently willing to shake up their infield to accommodate his talent.

While Priddy got his share of ink during the off-season, though, it was Rizzuto who garnered the most. During the winter months, the New York press regularly ran articles about the shortstop-to-be. It was only natural, perhaps, since Rizzuto was a hometown hero. Articles about the former Richmond Hill star ran often. In January, the *Saturday Evening Post* ran a big spread on him.

In the *New York Times*, Kansas City trainer Eddie Froelich said of Rizzuto,

> "He's just born to be a great player. Let's take him apart and judge him on his merits. First, his arm. What an arm! He can get the ball away as fast as Durocher ever did, and you know Durocher could do that better than any shortstop that ever lived.
>
> "As for his running, he is in some respects a better runner than Pee Wee Reese (comparisons between the two shortstops began in 1939 when Reese played for Louisville of the American Association; Reese was promoted to the Brooklyn Dodgers in 1940). He is a good slider. He breaks fast. He has split-second thinking, runs on his intuition and takes advantage of every opportunity. I've seen him tear around those bases in the best Cobb manner and score all the way from first on a single more than once on hit-and-run plays.
>
> "Now for his hitting power. That's where he obliterates the impression he is a little guy. You know how the fences run at

Kansas City. They are both 350 feet away at the foul lines. Well, those are the new fences. There's an old fence in left field, about 380 feet away, and I've seen Phil hit one that not only cleared the new fence but the old one, too. Now, don't get the impression he is a long hitter. Only once in a while. But he is really a sharp hitter. He hits to all fields, down the foul lines, between the fielder, and nobody knows how to pitch to him. One team used to throw high and inside to him. Another would slow up on him. Another would curve him. But it didn't help. He hit 'em all."

If there was anything about Rizzuto that had folks raising the red flag, it was his size. Rizzuto, well known at that point as either "The Flea" or "The Scooter," both in reference to his size, stood 5-foot-6 and weighed in the low 150s during his final minor league season. Compared to most major leaguers, Rizzuto was indeed a squirt, as some scribes referred to him.

"Everyone wonders about my size," he said to Arthur E. Patterson. "I've had a great deal of trouble convincing people I am a ballplayer—even some managers."

"Phil will look mighty small to the Yankee fans the first day they see him," warned Froelich. "He looked awfully small to me. After he hit a 370-foot triple to right field, I changed my mind. He got big overnight."

Ironically, when Rizzuto reported to the spring training base in February he had a heap of trouble trying to get in through the front door. Long-time clubhouse man Fred Logan looked at the pint-sized young man and told him to come back later for autographs. Pitcher Lefty Gomez finally intervened and Rizzuto walked into the clubhouse, awestruck, and took his locker between Bill Dickey and Red Ruffing. The experience left Rizzuto flustered.

"When I first saw those big guys down there at spring training, I didn't think I'd make it," Rizzuto admitted to Joe Trimble. "They were so darned big—DiMaggio, Henrich, and

Keller, Ruffing, Dickey, Lindell—all of them. I was really discouraged for quite a while."

Former Blues teammate Billy Hitchcock was sure that Rizzuto was ready for the major leagues, no matter what the New Yorker's size. "I didn't see how he could miss. He was small, but he could do everything. He had good hands. Phil never had a particularly strong arm but he got rid of the ball quick and at shortstop, you know, it's important to get rid of the ball quick. He could do that. He had good range. He was a good defensive shortstop, and of course, a good offensive player. He was a good hitter, a good bunter, an excellent bunter— he could run, and he didn't strike out much. Naturally he didn't have much power but he got the bat on the ball—he could handle the bat — and he could hit and run. I didn't know much about major league baseball at that time but I thought he was a sure major league ballplayer. I just figured he was a can't-miss because he could do everything well."

Stories of Rizzuto's exploits at Kansas City were aplenty and, of course, they reached New York, where manager Joe McCarthy heard them all. The Yankee pilot admitted to one writer in December 1940 that he'd heard so many "yarns" about Rizzuto, that he felt he had known the youngster for years.

For Rizzuto, New York would be a homecoming, even if he did grow up on the other side of the city. It was anything but a homecoming for Priddy, who was from Los Angeles. They were so good, that manager Joe McCarthy was ready to shake up his infield. Joe Gordon, considered the league's best second baseman in 1940, would be moved to either third base or first base to accommodate Priddy, while Rizzuto would take over at short, replacing the veteran Frank Crosetti. Gordon wasn't happy with the talk. Crosetti, a fine-fielding shortstop in his own right, had been the Yankee shortstop for most of the past nine years, teaming with the great Yankee second baseman, Tony Lazzeri, for many of them. Although a solid fielder—the reason he started for so many years— Crosetti's batting average left a lot to be desired. He batted a career-high .288 in 1936, but other than that season, rarely hit above .250. In 1939, Crosetti hit .233 and then dipped to .194—the lowest of any regular in the league—the following season. With Rizzuto ripping up the American Association, the 30-year-old Crosetti read the writing on the wall. Like a good Yankee, he was ready to accept his new status as a backup. Gordon was another matter entirely. During his first three years with the Yankees, "The Flash" had started 432 games at second base, beginning with his rookie year in 1938. In 1940 he hit .281, cracked 32 doubles, 10 triples, and 30 home runs and drove in 103 runs. In the field, he was regarded as exceptional, leading the league in assists with 505. Gordon reported to the St. Petersburg, Florida, camp on February 27, 1941, ready to sign but not particularly happy about the talk of his shift in the infield.

"Believe me, it was not easy for Gerry Priddy and me in the Yankee camp," Rizzuto recalled in *The Sporting News* in 1951. "For more than a week, the atmosphere was cold. I was after Frankie Crosetti's job, Priddy was aiming at Joe Gordon's."

To Rizzuto, an overly friendly sort, the rough treatment early on was hard to take, but he fully understood his position in the pecking order. But it didn't get any easier until Joe DiMaggio, for some unknown reason, took a liking to the kid. "I was coming to take Crosetti's job," he said in *Yankees Magazine*. "He was a big favorite. I wasn't exactly ostracized, but I wasn't accepted. I was having trouble getting into the batter's cage. After four or five days DiMaggio came over and said, 'Look, let the kid in there to take his turn.' That really broke the ice. Joe took me under his wing."

"Well, that was heaven to me," he recalled in *The Sporting News*. "The other players began to warm up to me. In fact, they warmed up to me much too eagerly. I started to be the butt of their tricks and jokes."

Taking DiMaggio's lead, other players, including Lefty Gomez, made Rizzuto feel comfortable. Veterans Bill Dickey and Red Ruffing also gave him immense support. So did a somewhat unlikely individual, Frank Crosetti.

"This is all very strange," Rizzuto said to Dan Daniel during the spring. "Ever since Crosetti came to New York I have been a Crosetti rooter. For years he has been my hero, my model. I used to sit in the stadium and note all of his actions and little mannerisms and then copy them. Even to hitching up his belt. And now they tell me I have a chance to win his position."

Crosetti, affectionately called "Crow" by his teammates, probably had a couple of years as a starter left in his career, if not in New York, then somewhere, but he latched onto his role as teacher. He showed Rizzuto the ropes of the major leagues.

"Crosetti was the same type of hitter I was and played the same way," Rizzuto said in *Yankees Magazine*. "He taught me how to get hit with the ball like he did, without getting hurt. And how to hit and run, and a couple of tricky plays with the bunt. (I got) a lot of extra base hits I'd never have gotten," without Crosetti's help. McCarthy, too, worked with Rizzuto, helping the youngster plant his feet better before throwing to first base. Even Gordon, as unhappy as he was with the impending moves, gave pointers to Priddy. After all, the common goal was to win the World Series, and Gordon was not about to rock the boat too much.

While the veteran Yankees gave Rizzuto the cold shoulder early on, they knew all about the kid from Glendale. "We knew all about Phil because he had been with Kansas City for a couple of years," says former Yankee outfielder Tommy Henrich. "We were aware of Gerry Priddy and Rizzuto. I was expecting a guy (Rizzuto) that was well-qualified to be a big league shortstop because he had already paid his dues. Yeah, man, we went through spring training and you could see Gerry Priddy and Rizzuto, what a combination. I could see that Rizzuto—everybody could see— that he was a young kid who could really cover the ground. He could play shortstop, no doubt about that.

"Oh, here and there you'd hear things about him that he was a naive little boy. But I knew he was from some little suburb outside of Brooklyn. As long as you are raised in

Brooklyn you're not naive. I knew that, but he played the part very well. He was the little boy. Early on when I got acquainted with Rizzuto I knew he knew what the heck to do. They played tricks on him and all that. I always felt in the back of my mind that Rizzuto was a true little son of a gun."

Perhaps driven by his fear of being benched, Rizzuto worked diligently to improve on his game under the hot Florida sun. Always a starter, Rizzuto did not know what he would do with himself if he had to be benched. "I am all keyed up, the nervous type," he said to Dan Daniel. "I've got to be out there doing something. I am afraid I never will get the poise which is Crosetti's. To get into half the games would be fine. To bury myself in the dugout— well, I can't even think of it. That would kill me."

Rizzuto, who missed some time due to a minor injury, had another concern that spring. In the winter, he had registered for the draft, like millions of other young men. That spring he got a letter from his draft board in New York to get his physical. Phil got the physical transferred to Florida, where he promptly passed it with flying colors. However, he was able to garner a 3-A classification before March was over. His classification meant that he was the main supporter of his family and therefore exempt from the draft. By then his father had lost his job with the transit company and was making only $20 a week as a part-time dock worker. His brother Al was also out of work and so, indeed, Phil, who had signed a contract calling for $5,000, was truly his family's bread-and-butter man.

Late in March, McCarthy made his official decision concerning his infield. Rizzuto and Priddy would make up his double play combination, Gordon would move to first base, and Red Rolfe would return to third base. Gordon replaced Babe Dahlgren, who batted a disappointing .264 at first. Rolfe, a starter since 1935, hit .250 the year before and whacked 10 homers. The outfield was set with Henrich, DiMaggio, and Charlie Keller. Both Keller and DiMaggio were coming off of solid seasons, while Henrich was pegged to replace George Selkirk. Dickey was behind the plate, with a pitching staff led by Gomez, Ruffing, Marius Russo, and Spud Chandler.

McCarthy was pleased with his decision, although he historically was leery of rookies and did take some heat from the press in the case of Gordon. But to the veteran manager, these were the moves that made the most sense. The manager was still fuming over the Yankees' third-place finish the year before, even if they were just two games back of the champion Detroit Tigers, and one behind the second-place Cleveland Indians. He was determined to get off to a quick start in 1941, even if it meant an overhaul of his infield. McCarthy sorely wanted New York to return to its glory of the previous few seasons, when the Yankees won an unprecedented four world championships in four straight seasons (1936-39). During that incredible run, New York averaged 102 wins a year, and won sixteen of nineteen World Series games (the great New York Giant pitcher Carl Hubbell won two of those games), beating the New York Giants twice (1936-37), and the Chicago Cubs (1938) and Cincinnati Reds (1939) once each. The Tigers, replacing the Yankees in the fall classic in 1940, were nipped by Cincinnati in seven games. And now McCarthy was ready to claim first place again.

By mid-April, as the Yankees prepared to play their annual three-game exhibition series with the Brooklyn Dodgers in New York, the starting lineup was now intact (well, almost; Priddy would miss the opening of the season because of an injury). Rizzuto, still learning the tools of his trade, had proven to McCarthy that he belonged at shortstop. After seeing "The Flea" for several weeks in Florida, Dan Daniel filed these words about Rizzuto:

> "There is every indication that Rizzuto is one of those fool-proof infielders. He comes to Flatbush (Ebbets Field) after a long layoff with a charley horse, with a batting average of .425 and many of the outstanding attributes of a splendid ballplayer.

In the field, Rizzuto has no weakness. He moves as fast and as far to his right as he does to his left. He is friendly to the center and left fielders, as he races out for anything that any shortstop ever took out of the air. On ground balls, he has a knack which few rookies display — the ability to take the ball deftly and consistently on the half-hop. On the base paths, the Flea is Speed."

Dan Daniel was right, and in a few days, The Flea was an official member of the New York Yankees major league baseball club.

"You never saw such big guys. Ruffing, Dickey, DiMaggio—even the bat boy looked like a tree top. Nobody paid me mind and I figured it was part of the initiation. But finally I began to worry that I had committed some boo-boo to get the ice treatment. Lefty Gomez looked like a nice sort, so I told him my troubles. Lefty told me, 'Relax, they're not snubbing you, they just haven't seen you yet.'"

—*Rookie Phil Rizzuto, New York Journal-American*

▪ 4 ▪

Rookie Rizzuto

With about 300 teachers and students from Richmond Hill High School and a score of Rizzutos among the 13,097 fans at Ebbets Field on April 11, 1941, Phil Rizzuto made his New York professional debut. Gerry Priddy, meanwhile, had suffered an ankle injury a few weeks earlier and would not only miss the Brooklyn series, but the start of the season. On the same day that the Germans were driving fiercely toward Yugoslavia as World War II heated up around the globe, Rizzuto was hitless in four at-bats as the Yankees played the Brooklyn Dodgers in the first game of a three-game exhibition series.

In the field, it was a shaky outing at best for the little guy who was expected to move in at shortstop. Rizzuto made four putouts, had three assists, but also muffed three plays, much to the chagrin of manager Joe McCarthy. Frank Crosetti simply watched from the bench and had words of encouragement for his replacement. Charlie Keller slammed two homers for the Yankees, including a blow in the ninth inning to give his team a 7-6 victory. The win ended a Brooklyn 11-game exhibition winning streak, and broke a four-game Yankee slide.

Even though the Dodgers had not won a pennant in 21 years, the rivalry between the two clubs was heavy and filtered down to their fans. It was no surprise then, when tempers flared over a foul ball. According to *The New York Times*, the game was interrupted briefly when a fight erupted between fans and ushers during the contest. "An usher raced for the (foul) ball and, annoyed at just missing it, took issue with the youth in the box. Another young man joined in the fray, and shortly an army of ushers and fans were embroiled. The first usher tore a sweater from the back of one fan but, so far as could be observed, the ball remained in the hands of the boy who snatched it."

The Yankees won the next day, nipping the Dodgers again at their home park, 3-2. It was a bitter cold day for the 18,834 fans in attendance, a few of whom built a fire behind the Yankee dugout in the eighth inning. Joe DiMaggio's ninth-inning double off Ed Head brought home Tommy Henrich with the winning run. The blast, off the left-centerfield wall, was a few feet away from where Keller's game-winning home run had hit the day before. For Phil Rizzuto, though, it was another frustrating day at the plate; he went 0-for-5. In the field, he handled three chances flawlessly. Seeing that Rizzuto was playing tight as he tried to make a big splash, Yankee pitcher Lefty Gomez broke up the rookie midway through the game. With the bases loaded with Dodgers, Gomez waved to Rizzuto to come to the pitcher's mound for a conference. "Why is he calling me, I wondered," Rizzuto said years later during a television interview. "I go in and he says to me, 'Are your mom and pop here?' I told him yes, and he said, 'Well, now they can say the great Lefty Gomez called on their son for an important conference.' Lefty Gomez was a very funny man."

On April 13, when Russia and Japan signed a neutrality treaty and the Germans pushed into Egypt, Rizzuto finally broke out of his slump in the third game as the Yankees swept the Ebbets Field series with a 3-0 shutout. The shortstop whacked two hits in four trips, made four putouts and added five assists in the field. Rizzuto played a role in two of the Yankees' seven double plays. Ernie Bonham and Atley Donald combined on a two-hitter before 16,531 fans, as manager Joe McCarthy sat in the dugout in his "civvies."

And so, as the exhibition season came to an end, Rizzuto and the Yankees found themselves 7-5 favorites to win the American League pennant. Rizzuto knew, however, that he had to play better than he did against Brooklyn. In the three games, he had just two hits in 13 at-bats. While there may have been some concern on Rizzuto's part, his teammates were not particularly worried.

The exhibition series was to offer the fans and press a chance to begin their quest to decide who was better — Reese or Rizzuto. The two last faced each other in 1939 in the American Association, with Rizzuto getting the better of it statistically. Reese got the call to the major leagues, not necesarily because he was better than Rizzuto, but because the Dodgers needed a shortstop. The "duel" never materialized in April, though, because Reese missed the series with a heel injury.

"Our careers kind of paralleled," says Reese. "I played against Phil in the Association. He played with Kansas City and I was with the Louisville Colonels. I played against him in 1939. They had a great ball club. They had quite a few people who went up and played with the Yankees. Later we played in the service together overseas in a series between the Navy and Army. And of course we played against each other in the World Series. I know I didn't make a big deal of who was better, and I don't think Phil did either. That made good copy for the press. The only thing I wanted to do all those years was to beat the Yankees. I wasn't concerned whether or not I was outplaying Phil."

Originally, Reese's contract was owned by the Boston Red Sox. According to David Halberstam, in his book *Summer of '49*, team owner Tom Yawkey had bought the Colonels for $195,000 just so he could own the rights to Reese. Midway through the 1939 season, however, reportedly as a result of pressure from Red Sox player-manager Joe Cronin, the team's shortstop, he was sold to the Dodgers for $75,000. Cronin, apparently concerned for his own job, was not about to bring up a young kid with obvious talent who could take away several years of his playing career.

After defeating the Dodgers, the Yankees boarded a train for Washington, D.C., and the season-opener against the Senators. By the time the Bronx Bombers got up the next morning, four people had died and two inmates were captured during an attempted prison break at Sing Sing in Ossining, New York, the worst prison break the facility had ever known. That was the topic of discussion at breakfast that morning as the Yankees sought to regain possession of the top spot in the American League from Detroit.

Thirty-three thousand fans packed Griffith Stadium on a beautiful, yet steamy, summer-like afternoon. Before the game started, Rizzuto and Priddy, the two heralded rookies, got a surprise. As described in *The New York Times*, "Events leading to the inaugural ceremonies began shortly before 2:30 when, by way of letting the sweltering crowd know something was about to happen, a huge floral horseshoe was wheeled out to the center of the diamond. It was a gift to Gerald Priddy and Phil Rizzuto, the Yanks' newly welded second-base combination, from the fans of Norfolk, Virginia, where this pair of youngsters performed in 1938." Actually, there were gifts, and many of them. When the pair opened up the packages after the game they found clothes, portable radios, candy, books, shaving kits, and more.

Rizzuto was starry-eyed shortly thereafter when Franklin D. Roosevelt made his way into the ballpark for the traditional throwing out of the first ball. "Soon came a final group of special police and secret service men and then, in full view, rolled the big, open touring car, from the rear seat of which beamed the famous Rooseveltian smile while the most famous fedora in the nation waved gaily to the cheering crowd," *The New York Times* reported. "As the President entered his box alongside the Senators' dugout the band struck up 'The Star-Spangled Banner,' more cheers followed and the remainder of the program moved with amazing swiftness."

The article continued, "Back to home plate marched the band, while the players, who, either through accident or design, had never moved off their respective foul lines, broke ranks and grouped in front of the Presidential box for the time-honored first toss of the season. After an interminable number of feints for the benefit of news photographers Mr. Roosevelt finally sent the ball flying into the scrambling mass of ballplayers. This contest, at least, went to the Senators. Out of the melee Arnold Anderson, rookie pitcher, bobbed up as proud possessor of the ball that officially launched the 1941 campaign." As for Rizzuto, he simply said at the time, that it was "quite a thrill."

It was not a thrill for the Senators once the game started. Yankee lefthander Marius Russo hurled a three-hitter in shutting out the home team, 3-0. Rizzuto batted leadoff and was hitless in four at-bats. In the field, he had a putout and four assists. Rizzuto got another thrill the next morning, though, when *The New York Times* ran a photo of him at the plate, taking the first pitch of the 1941 season.

Immediately after the Washington game, the Yankees were on a train again, this time back to New York and Yankee Stadium for their home opener the next day. Rizzuto slept at home, of course, and recalled his first trip to the Stadium as a bonafide major leaguer the morning of the game.

"I had driven my ten-year old Ford up to the Stadium that morning," he told Joe Trimble. "It was a real jalopy—what the kids today call 'hot-rods.' It was a convertible at one time but was strictly an open-air chariot by the time I got it. There was no windshield, the canvas top was in ribbons, I had pinup pictures of Hollywood babes pasted on the dashboard and even had fur tails flying from the hood. There was only one parking place left when I arrived, right between two big, beautiful cars. One was Ruffing's Cadillac and the other was Gomez's La Salle. I guess someone told Barrow about it, because I got the devil from him." Barrow told Rizzuto to get the car out of the lot that day and never bring it back. Rizzuto never did.

With 40,128 people in attendance, New York lost its home opener, 3-1, to the Philadelphia Athletics on April 15. Rizzuto again went hitless, going 0-3 with four assists and three putouts.

The next day Rizzuto hit paydirt, cracking three hits, including a double that brought the crowd of 8,004 to its feet when he slid headfirst into second base. Rizzuto also scored a run and drove in another. Weakened by a five-run Philadelphia sixth inning, the Yankees lost the game, 10-7. Rizzuto continued to hit the next day, getting two hits in a 9-4 Yankee win over the A's. Among the two hits was Rizzuto's first major league bunt single, the first of many to come that year and beyond. Now healed from his injury, Priddy joined Rizzuto in the field, moving in at second base, with Joe Gordon going to first base.

Although the Yankees were ripped by Washington the next day, 7-4, Rizzuto again hit with precision. He had two hits in four at-bats, including a triple. In the field, though, he made two errors. In a close play at second base, Rizzuto accidentally spiked Cecil Travis in the first inning, causing the Senators' shortstop to leave the game. Rizzuto capped his rookie week with a two-hit game the next day. But in the field, he made another error. The Yankees, behind Joe DiMaggio's 10th-inning home run, defeated the Senators, 5-2. The 10th-inning rally was sparked by Rizzuto, who led off with a triple to the rightfield corner. Red Rolfe knocked in Rizzuto with a single and, two batters later, DiMaggio slugged his second homer of the young season.

Through one week of major league ball, Rizzuto was 9-for-25 with three runs scored, two triples, one double, and one RBI. In the field, he had six putouts, 12 assists, and three errors. The Yankees were 3-3, behind first-place Boston and Cleveland. By the end of April, Rizzuto had passed the early tests at the plate, although the jury was still out on whether the youngster could handle the big time in the field.

"How good is he?" asked sports writer Herbert Goren in his column. "Can he run and throw with Reese? Can he hit with Miller (Eddie Miller of the Boston Braves)? What does he do best?"

Goren responded to his own questions. "The answers as yet are incomplete. Rizzuto has shown aptitudes in all directions. He is an exciting performer and a real competitor, with the spirit of a sandlotter. He is eager to meet up with the best that others can throw against him; impatient to play against the Tigers and Indians, to bat against Newsom and Feller.

"Phil has functioned best on double plays, either in starting them or in pivoting; and has yet to make a bad throw to second base. He has speeded up the team double play production tremendously.

"McCarthy has detected only one fault with Rizzuto's play; it cropped up in Washington. A ground ball was hit to his right and, instead of cutting sharply and taking it on a short hop, he went back for it and his throw was hurried, late and wide. The manager told him about it that night. Rizzuto understood. McCarthy called it a mark of inexperience and said he doubted Rizzuto would make many such mistakes in a season."

Taking into account Rizzuto's hitting through the first week and in spring training, Goren wrote that the rookie "appears capable of hitting .300. Rizzuto is a versatile batter. His hits have fallen everywhere, down the foul lines, between the outfielders, once over the centerfielder's head for three bases, once through the middle over second base into centerfield. He has beaten out a half dozen bunts and belted a homer into the left field seats at the Stadium, a drive of more than 400 feet. All the pitchers have been able to discover about him is that he gets most of his power on pitches that are high and inside. But he has hit everything else, too. His diminutive size makes him that much harder to fool. His speed and bunting ability also are in his favor. Though he never led off until this year, he has managed to get on much more frequently than Frankie Crosetti ever did."

Mel Allen, who had joined the Yankees two years earlier as a broadcaster, remembers Rizzuto in those first few weeks. "Nobody had a real perception of him until he took over for Crosetti. He did an excellent job of leading off. He was short to begin with and most people's reactions to a smaller guy is greater, especially at the outset. He could bunt, he could steal a base. He could range well at shortstop. He got rid of the ball quickly, although he didn't have a strong arm. But he made the double play."

Less than a month into the season, Rizzuto was being compared with Lou Boudreau and Luke Appling, two outstanding veterans, as well as to Reese and Miller. Appling, Boudreau, and Reese eventually made it into the Hall of Fame, while Miller proved to be nothing more than a flash phenom, paling miserably in comparison to Rizzuto's career numbers.

Within a couple of weeks of Goren's "report card," Rizzuto's status, as well as the Yankees', fell considerably. On the morning of May 12, while London was being hit hard by the Nazis, New York was in fourth place with a record of 14-11, behind first-place Cleveland, Boston, and Chicago. On May 13th, when the Nazis declared the Red Sea a war zone, the Yankees lost to Bob Feller and the Indians, 2-1, in 10 innings. Now the Yankees were 14-13. Rizzuto doubled (his only hit in five at-bats) and scored the Yanks' only run. The Indians swept the series the next day, winning 4-1. It was the New Yorkers' fourth straight loss. Even though Rizzuto had a hit and nearly hit a home run, McCarthy was considering changes in the lineup. Specifically, he felt that both Priddy and Rizzuto were pressing too hard. At the plate, Rizzuto had become inconsistent, and in the field, his errors were driving McCarthy crazy. "Soon my throwing became worse and I started pressing more and more, until I lost my confidence to throw out any runner," admitted Rizzuto in a story he wrote with Milton Gross for the *Saturday Evening Post* years later.

McCarthy was also concerned because, the year before, the Yankees got off to a sluggish start and lost out on the pennant. The cigar-puffing McCarthy wanted to derail that same scenario as soon as possible, and when it didn't get any better the next afternoon, he decided to spring into action. The Yankees fell below .500 that day (May 15) when they lost to Chicago, 13-1. Now McCarthy had seen enough as his mighty Yankees fell to the middle of the standings. McCarthy had his third-base coach and No. 1 assistant Art Fletcher fetch first Priddy, then Rizzuto. Underneath the stands the manager explained to the slumping duo of Rizzuto and Priddy that they were being benched. Rizzuto was stunned, even after Priddy came back out onto the field and told his teammate of his fate.

Rizzuto never imagined he'd be relegated to the bench. "I really didn't think I was due for the same medicine," Rizzuto told Trimble. "I knew the team wasn't going good but I felt that I was just hitting my stride and that we would soon get off on a three- or four-game winning streak which would cure all our troubles. It was the first time that I'd ever been benched and I had a sinking feeling in my stomach. I pleaded with him to let me stay in the lineup but he shook his head firmly." McCarthy called on Crosetti to move back to shortstop and Joe Gordon to second. Johnny Sturm replaced Gordon at first base. At the time, Rizzuto was down to .246, and Priddy was at .204.

"McCarthy put Priddy at second base and put Joe Gordon at first base. He thought he was going to have the greatest infield in the history of baseball," recalls Tommy Henrich. "As it turned out, Gordon wasn't a very good first baseman and Priddy wasn't ready to play good ball at second base. McCarthy had to take Priddy out and put Gordon at second and they brought in Johnny Sturm, who played very well for us. He was no star, but he played to his potential all year long. Although Rizzuto was benched for a while, too, he eventually played up to his potential and didn't allow the big-league jitters to get to him at all. But Priddy did. It wasn't surprising to me because Phil was a pretty cute and calculating guy at a young age. He knew his way around. Let's put it that way."

At the time, though, Rizzuto did not know what the future held for him. As for the lineup changes, they paid off, at least in the final score, immediately. The Yankees finally broke the five-game losing streak with a 6-5 win over Chicago. To the kid from Glendale, it was tough to take his demotion, and he thought his career was in jeopardy.

"Things went sour from the start," Rizzuto said in *The Sporting News*, ignoring the fact that he played quite well for the first few weeks of the season. "Priddy and I were benched. I decided that I would have to spend the season on the bench." Devastated at first, Rizzuto finally realized what McCarthy was up to, which was to give the youngster some time to sit back and gain some experience from the vantage point of the bench.

"He (McCarthy) would point out things that Crosetti was doing," says Mel Allen. "Joe McCarthy was smart in spoon-feeding Phil, letting him adjust to the major leagues."

Rizzuto also learned that he and Priddy were not the first rookies to see the bench after starting the season in the lineup. Gordon had the same fate, and so had many others. In addition, Phil was told by the other players how tight he was playing and how obvious it was that he was pressing too hard. Looking at the total picture, Rizzuto began to realize that they were right, that he was trying too hard, that he was replaying every play of that day's game in his mind.

With Crosetti in the lineup at short, Gordon at second, and Sturm at first, the Yankees became consistent and began to make their move in the standings. On June 15, as 43,962 watched at the stadium, the Yankees won their seventh straight game, 3-2 over the Indians. By June 16, the Yankees were 32-22, winning 18 of 25 games, and were now only two games back of first-place Cleveland. Crosetti, who started like a house of fire, had tailed off, but there was no denying the team's success with him in the lineup.   With the way things were going, there seemed little chance that Rizzuto would be back in the lineup any time soon.

Two days later, the front-page headlines told of the United States' declaration that all Nazi consulates be closed in the country; across the Atlantic Ocean, the British opened a heavy offensive in Libya. In the sports section, Joe DiMaggio's fifth-inning double in a 6-4 win over Cleveland extended his hitting streak to 29 games, tying the team record shared by Indians manager Roger Peckinpaugh and Earle Combs. In the second inning, however, the Yankees had a setback. Crosetti's middle finger on his left hand was accidentally spiked by Hal Trosky, who was out sliding into the bag at second base. The injury required two stitches and put Crosetti on the bench for at least five days.

Rizzuto immediately took advantage of the situation, rapped two hits in three at-bats, scored two runs, and in the field recorded four assists as the Yankees moved to within one game of first place. It was an eighth-inning walk to Rizzuto that helped spark a three-run burst that ultimately led to the 6-4 decision.

"If Crosetti, batting .350 (actually .237) at the time, had not been spiked, what would have happened to me?" Rizzuto wondered in *The Sporting News*. But "Trosky spiked Crosetti in the hand. I was sent to short."

For the next few days, the Yankees did not do very well, losing two to the White Sox, 8-7 and 3-2, despite DiMaggio's now 31-game hitting streak. Rizzuto, though, hacked three hits in the two contests, scoring a run and driving in two. In the 8-7 loss, Rizzuto was nipped at the plate late in the game with what would have been the tying run. At that point, it didn't seem to matter. McCarthy was happy to have Rizzuto back in the lineup, even if he didn't let the kid know. The day after Joe Louis stopped Billy Conn in 13 rounds to hold onto his heavyweight crown, June 19, Rizzuto, batting eighth regularly now, banged out two more hits, as the Yankees broke the short skid with a 7-2 win over Chicago. When the Sunday papers came out that week, they showed Ted Williams of Boston leading the American League in hitting with a .420 batting average. Down lower, Rizzuto stood at .258 with one home run, 10 RBIs, and 23 runs scored. Crosetti had leveled off at .237, with a homer and 13 RBIs, and just seven runs scored.

During this time, DiMaggio's hitting streak was not the only Yankee record setter. Heading into its June 21 game with

Detroit, New York had homered in 16 straight contests. One more and the Yanks would tie Detroit for the major league record. It appeared as if that record—and the game—was slipping away as it went into the seventh inning. Then, the unlikeliest of Yankees, Phil Rizzuto, powered a home run. The homer streak remained alive, even if the Yankees could not win the game. It was New York's 28th home run in that span, a record in itself. Meanwhile, DiMaggio ran his streak to 34 in a row, six away from Ty Cobb, and seven from George Sisler, for the modern-day mark.

The next day, DiMaggio kept both streaks alive, smacking his 15th homer of the season as New York beat Detroit. Elsewhere, Cleveland stayed two up when Bob Feller won his 10th game of the year, 6-0 over Washington. Two days later, the Yankees moved to within one game of first by knocking off the St. Louis Browns, 9-1, while Cleveland was getting doused by Boston, 13-2.

With DiMaggio unstoppable, a homer barrage of incredible proportions, and Rizzuto getting closer and closer to .300, the Yankees were on fire. On June 25 they moved into a virtual first-place tie with Cleveland, with Rizzuto's smash through the middle driving in the decisive run in a three-run eighth inning of a 7-5 victory over the Browns. The win gave New York a 38-25 record, actually putting them percentage points ahead of Cleveland, the first time since April 25th that the Yankees were atop the standings. In just a bit over a month, the Yankees had picked up nearly a dozen games on Cleveland.

For a while, the Yankees flip-flopped between first and second place. Most of the attention at this point centered on DiMaggio. On June 27 he extended his hitting streak to 39 in a row. And then, on June 29, DiMaggio had hits in both ends of a doubleheader with Boston to go to 42 straight, breaking Cobb's and Sisler's records on the same day. Only Willie Keeler's record of 44 in a row remained. Rizzuto had a good doubleheader, too, slugging four hits as New York won two to take a 1 1/2- game lead over Cleveland. From here on, it would be a one-team race, with New York taking control of the pennant run, hands down.

By mid-July, DiMaggio had broken Keeler's record, the Yankees had their team homer streak end after 25 games, and the Bronx Bombers were five ahead of Cleveland. As of July 12, Rizzuto was up to .305 with two home runs, 17 RBIs, and 32 runs scored. On July 13, when DiMaggio was extending his hitting streak to 53 consecutive games, Rizzuto had a 16-game batting streak of his own stopped in the second game of a doubleheader. DiMaggio reached 55 on July 15 and hit 56 on the 17th against Cleveland. The next day, DiMaggio's remarkable streak came to an end against the Indians. For the rookie Rizzuto, it was as great a run for him as it was for DiMaggio. As early as spring training, Rizzuto felt a special tie to the great centerfielder.

Rizzuto recalled in a *New York Post* interview years later, "In those days, the older guys took BP first, then the scrubeenies. Well, every time I got in the cage someone else would step in front of me. It went on for four or five days until DiMaggio finally said, 'Hey, let him hit.'

"After that we had a great relationship. I guess it was because I knew when to keep quiet. Joe was an introvert, he spoke very little. He loved movies and he'd ask me to go with him. Here I was, a rookie. I was in such awe of him I used to watch him shave—and then copy him." On the day the streak ended, however, Rizzuto's relationship with DiMaggio changed from one of awe to one of equality. "Joe kind of changed after that night," he continued. "He was real quiet and he asked me to walk back to the hotel with him. But halfway there he stopped in a bar. I started to follow him in, but he turned and said, 'No. I want to be alone.' The next day Joe was like a different person, like there was a tremendous weight off his shoulders. He was relaxed again, and he became one of the guys. That's the day I was no longer in awe of him. I guess that's when we became true friends."

By the end of July, Rizzuto was hitting .322 and the Yankees were 11 1/2 games in front of fading Cleveland. In mid-

August, the Yankees, with Rizzuto hitting second in the order, increased their lead to 15 games, with Chicago now in second place.

Late in the month, though, Rizzuto —and the Yankees— were in a mild slump. Once again showing that he didn't take slumps lightly, McCarthy sprang into action and despite the huge lead, made some changes. He put Priddy in at first, Crosetti at third, Frenchy Bordagaray in rightfield, and Ken Silvestri behind the plate. All were short-term moves, but naturally, the Yankees responded, beating up the Indians, 7-2. By then, Rizzuto's job was secure, and he was relieved that he wasn't put on the bench. At the time, he was batting .314, with 45 runs, 37 RBIs and 10 stolen bases.

Only September lay ahead, with the Yankees looking forward to a run that would feature a massive number of home games. The schedule did not let them down as the Yankees coasted to the pennant, 17 games ahead of Boston, 24 over Chicago. Cleveland and Detroit were tied for fourth place, well out of contention. With 18 games remaining on their schedule, the Yankees clinched the pennant on September 4, the earliest clinching date in history to that time.

On the final day of the regular season, September 28, the Yankees scored a 6-0 victory over Washington to go 101-53. Meanwhile, on the other side of the city, Brooklyn was winning its first pennant since 1920. It wasn't as easy for the Dodgers, who battled the St. Louis Cardinals until the last week of the season. In the end, the Dodgers won 100 games and lost 54 to edge Billy Southworth's Cards by three games. The Dodgers had a reputation that season as a bunch of loudmouths, led by their manager, Leo "The Lip" Durocher, and the general manager, Larry MacPhail, a calculating executive who was the ultimate promoter. Several times during the year Durocher was booted from games by fed-up umpires. The Yankees, of course, were quiet, proven winners.

It was no surprise, therefore, that the World Series matchup was a big topic at the Polo Grounds on September 30, the night when Joe Louis knocked out Lou Nova in the sixth round to retain his heavyweight title. It was also the topic of ticket scalpers, who fell into a gold mine when Brooklyn won the pennant. Many of them had secured blocks of tickets during the latter part of the season. When it turned out that Brooklyn would be the Yankees' opponent, the Subway Series dream became a reality and ticket interest was great. It was no surprise when scalpers began asking for large sums of money per ticket. Disgruntled fans, unable to pay the high prices, would have to be content listening to the games on the radio.

When the final pitch had been thrown that regular season, it showed Rizzuto with a .307 batting average, with 20 doubles, nine triples, three home runs, 65 runs, 46 RBIs, and 14 stolen bases. In the field, Rizzuto played a big part in the team's 194 double plays, which tied the major league mark for a season (held by Cincinnati). In one game, Rizzuto teamed with Gordon on seven double plays. Rizzuto, however, finished with a fielding percentage of just .957, his worst figure as a full-time regular (in 1955 he had a .957 in 79 games, and he fielded .934 in 1956 in 30 games).

In the World Series, Rizzuto—somewhat nervous over playing in the classic, in part because it was his first, in part because he knew he would be in the center of it all at shortstop — handled 30 of 31 chances flawlessly. At the plate, he slumped, getting just two singles in 18 at-bats. With Gordon, Keller, Sturm, Rolfe, and DiMaggio banging the ball all over the place, though, it didn't matter. New York won the series in five games. Brooklyn, which hadn't been in a World Series in 21 years, did make for a worthy opponent, even if it fell short. With the fiery Durocher leading the way from the bench, the Dodgers played hard-nosed ball, using the second-base area as a launching ground. With American League umpires Bill McGowan and Bill Grieve and National League umpires Larry Goetz and Babe Pinelli seemingly oblivious to the roughhouse tactics around the second sack, the Dodgers started the assault and the Yankees retaliated.

Soon, the middle of the infield resembled a Civil War battleground, with bodies crashing and spikes flying, with Rizzuto and Gordon of the Yankees, and Reese and Billy Herman and Pete Coscarart (the latter replaced Herman at second base for Brooklyn when Herman pulled a muscle in the third game) in the thick of the action. In turn, pitchers began throwing at batters. Clearly, it was not advisable for any player to let down his guard in this series.

Considering how Reese and Rizzuto had been compared over the year, it was probably no coincidence that the second-base area became the heated zone it did. Reese, in his second year with Brooklyn, was really no match for Rizzuto statistically; however, Dodger fans made a case for him. The native of Kentucky hit just .229 with two homers and 46 RBIs. His fielding average of .946 paled in comparison to Rizzuto. In head-to-head competition, Rizzuto came out ahead back in 1939 when the two were in the minors.

That year Rizzuto batted .316 with 64 RBIs while Reese hit .279 with 57 RBIs. Rizzuto had a .944 fielding percentage to Reese's .943. Even then—although not as much as when they were both in New York — they were under the microscope as far as the media and fans were concerned. In 1940, by the way, Reese shared time with Durocher at short. He played in 84 games and batted .272 with five home runs and 28 RBIs. The former American Association rivals were now with the big boys, and comparisons were inevitable in the hot New York market.

The World Series opened at Yankee Stadium on October 1 under cloudy skies. The teams split the first two games. There were 68,540 fans in the stands for the opener, in which Ruffing shut down Brooklyn, 3-2. Rizzuto was hitless in four at-bats, hitting in the No. 8 spot. Brooklyn got a good pitching effort out of Whitlow Wyatt and the Dodgers won, 3-2. (Wyatt would nearly come to blows with DiMaggio in the fifth and final game after throwing a duster at the great Yankee's head. DiMaggio responded by whacking a screaming liner back at the box that sailed over Wyatt's head).

In the third game, Russo played a key role in the New York win, both at the plate and on the mound. Batting in the seventh inning, Russo slammed a ball off opposing pitcher Fred Fitzsimmons's right knee (the ball popped into the air and Reese caught it on the fly for the out) and forced the starter from the game. The Yankees immediately pushed across a run in the eighth off reliever Hugh Casey and won the game, 2-1.

But the 1941 World Series will be forever remembered for Mickey Owen's muff in the ninth inning of the fourth game. It was one of the most memorable events in the history of the World Series. With the Yankees leading the series, 2-1 but trailing this game, 4-3 Casey, back on the mound, seemed to have the game in hand, getting two quick outs. And it seemed to be over when Tommy Henrich missed badly on a two-strike pitch. The Ebbetts Field crowd went wild as the game appeared to be over. In the commotion, though, Owen could not handle the pitch and it rolled toward the backstop. Henrich raced safely to first base as fans poured onto the field.

When play was finally resumed, the Yankees were still alive. DiMaggio cracked a single, and Keller crushed a double into the screen in right field that scored both Henrich and DiMaggio. Bill Dickey was intentionally walked, but the move backfired when Gordon slugged a double to score two more runs. Rizzuto walked to load the bases again, but Yankee relief pitcher Johnny Murphy made an out to end the inning. The Yankees had scored four runs for one of the most improbable wins in World Series history. The Dodgers went down easily in their half of the ninth. New York won the game, 7-4, and now led the series, three games to one.

"I was just as popeyed and excited as anyone —I didn't even see Owen miss the ball," Rizzuto related to Joe Trimble. "I had my glove and Keller's and DiMag's in my hand. I stood at the end of the dugout, ready to rush down to the clubhouse under the stands. I thought the game was over when the big shout went up because I had seen Tommy miss his swing. I was halfway down the dugout steps toward the alley leading to the locker room when I heard the shouting from our bench and turned around to find people running all over the field and Henrich on first base."

The Yankees clinched the series the next day, October 6, with a 3-1 win, with Ernie Bonham picking up the victory. The Yankees had returned to the top at the expense of their crosstown rivals. It would also mark the beginning of several meetings between the two teams in the World Series in the following years, most of which would end in hard luck for the Dodgers.

Rizzuto didn't play a major role in the series victory, at least not at the plate, but he did hold his own at shortstop. Reese, meanwhile, didn't fare much better at the plate. He had just four hits—three of which came in the first game — in 20 at-bats, and was charged with three errors. Rizzuto, who took home $5,000 —matching his salary for the year—as the winners' share, wasn't concerned with the comparisons, though. The kid from Glendale was just thrilled to be a part of it all, especially when he realized that back in May, he had thought his career might be over.

And so, when the season was all said and done, even Rizzuto (who was unofficially selected by the sports writers as the American League's Rookie of the Year; there was no formal award at the time) believed that McCarthy's benching of him early in the year was a key to the successful campaign. Certainly it was that decision, and many more, that earned Rizzuto's respect for McCarthy: "He was the greatest manager I ever played for," Rizzuto said in *Yankees Magazine*. "He knew how to handle everybody. Some you had to give a kick in the backside, others a pat on the back, others you had to talk to. He'd never embarrass you in front of other players like some managers do. If you were to make a bad play, not an error but a bad throw to the wrong base, or miss a hit-and-run sign, when the inning was over he'd take you back to his office and tell you. He always wanted you to think, sleep, and drink baseball 24 hours a day."

Indeed, Rizzuto ate, slept, and drank baseball during his rookie season, a season that proved to everyone in baseball that he truly belonged.

"I remember one day I found a stool under my shower. Lefty Gomez said, 'Phil, better leave it there. Without the stool, the hot water takes so long to reach you, it is cold.'"

Phil Rizzuto, The Sporting News

Reflections on a Rookie Year

"They Made Me a Big Leaguer"
By Phil Rizzuto

As told to Milton Gross for Baseball Digest, 1946
Condensed from the Saturday Evening Post

I left home five years ago to take my first spring training at St. Petersburg, Florida with the New York Yankees. I was excited and scared, too; as scared as you would be if all the baseball you'd ever had was just four years in the minor leagues. I arrived at St. Pete a couple of days before the other infielders and outfielders. I don't think I'll ever forget my first look at Miller Huggins Field. It was green and inviting and lonely. The morning workout for pitchers was over. I walked over the shortstop area I hoped to patrol, and then, without much assurance, headed for the locker room.

"Outside, you. No kids allowed in here now." It was Fred Logan, the clubhouse man.

I started to tell him who I was when Lefty Gomez walked over. He had a towel wrapped around his middle and on his face a grin that I came to appreciate more and more as the season went along.

"G'wan, Fred," he said. "Don't you know who this cockroach is? " Then he turned to me and added, "C'mon in, Phil, before the ducks start stepping all over you."

That was my initiation.

I looked around the room for my locker and found it. There was my name right between Bill Dickey's and Red Ruffing's. It was enough to make me want to turn and run. I knew the fellows talked to each other while they were getting into uniform and undressing after workouts. What could I have to say to Bill and Red? But in the next few days I was wondering what I had ever been scared about. Any time I found myself wishing I knew the answer to one of Dickey's incessant riddles, there was Gomez cracking one of his jokes or Ruffing asking, "What's a six-letter word for an open bottle?"

It was a bit more difficult with manager Joe McCarthy, who'd take his position back of first base, from where he'd watch us work in the infield.

He didn't seem to be looking at anybody in particular, but I couldn't rid myself of the feeling that his eyes were taking in everything I did. They were, too.

One day he came over to me and said, "Can you do a buck-and-wing dance?"

"Sure," I replied, grinning like a fool.

"I don't mean on the dance floor," Joe said; "I mean on the ball field."

He showed me what he meant, in little dancing steps at shortstop. I wasn't making the play right in going after ground balls. He kept me practicing those prancing steps until I could field the ball without wasted time and motion. Later Joe Gordon, the best second baseman in baseball today, said, "You'll be surprised how that buck-and-wing will help you get into position for the grounder and the throw to first base. When I first came to spring training, that was one of the first things he taught me."

This was just the start of my fielding education. On balls hit to deep short I had always jammed my spikes into the ground before stooping to pick up the grounders. McCarthy spotted this immediately and made me let my right foot slide to a stop, so that I would be in a better balanced position to make the play and throw. McCarthy had Gordon demonstrate the techniques to me over and over again, all through the spring and even after we started North. They'd made me play toward second base while our coaches, Fletcher and Schulte, hit the ball between the short-stop hole and third base, so that I'd be forced to go all the way to my right to make the play. Then they went to work on my throwing and insisted that I throw overhand, instead of sidearm, the way Frank Crosetti does.

My throwing was to plague me for many weeks after the season opened, because I was scared and didn't realize there was little reason to hasten a throw for fast men, like George Case, then of Washington, for example.

The first time we played against Washington, Case, in his first time at bat, hit a ground ball to me. While he was coming to bat I kept saying to myself, 'Be ready. If he hits one down here, rush it.' I rushed it and didn't even get a grip on the ball before attempting to throw. Soon my throwing became worse and I started pressing more and more, until I lost my confidence to throw out any runner, let alone a swifty like Case.

Then Gordon and Crosetti took me in hand. "There's no need to rush your throws," they told me. "Take your time. You'll be surprised how much time you have for even the fastest man in the league, unless, of course, he catches you flat-footed."

I soon discovered that in the American League, just as in the American Association, a thrown ball is always faster than a man running. I started easing up, getting a better grip on the ball and a greater accuracy.

I don't know who helped me most my first year with the Yankees. No matter how I'd answer that, I'd be doing an injustice to some of the fellows who helped me. There were, for instance, the invaluable benefits derived from playing between Gordon and Red Rolfe. From the beginning they started shifting me around to get me into position for each hitter. I don't believe there were two batters for whom I played in the same position at their direction. The shifting continued even after we'd been around the circuit and I thought I had learned how to play hitters. Red and Trig knew each hitter as they did their own faces.

It really was a revelation to watch Gordon play the hitters. Trig is like Joe Di; you never realize how fast he really is and how much ground he can cover. With those long legs, you think he's just idling along, but I never saw anybody who could cover so much ground so fast and get into the correct position for his throw. He has an amazing baseball sense.

But it wasn't just individuals that made my first year with the Yankees so swell; it was the team itself, and its attitude. Here was I, a rookie, discovering every day how little I really knew about inside baseball and even about the mechanics of the game. Here was Crosetti, a great shortstop, helping me out every day — helping me so that I could take his job away from him. Before each game Frank would come from the dugout and make suggestions. "Step in a few feet," he'd say; or "Go more to your left." Every move I'd make on Frank's suggestions was an improvement to my playing.

"You'll break a finger sliding into a base that way," Frank pointed out to me one day as he watched me hook-sliding into second. "You let your hands drag along the ground as you hit it. Keep your hands in the air as you take the leap into the base. There's one sure way of doing it. When you reach first base, bend over and take a handful of dirt in each of your fists. All the time you're on base keep that dirt clenched in your fists. When you slide into second you'll find that your hands naturally will be held in the air because they are clenched over the dirt."

I tried it and he was right. I know DiMaggio followed the same system, but he failed to once and sprained a wrist late in the season. Favoring that sprained wrist, Joe later injured an ankle in Detroit and had to stay out of the game several weeks.

There probably wasn't a single phase of baseball Crosetti didn't touch on in giving me suggestions. Hitting? All I did at the beginning was come up to the plate and try to pull the ball. It got so bad that one day in Washington the Senators' infield pulled over to the left, giving me the entire right field corner. All I had to do was punch into right, but it remained for Crosetti and McCarthy to point out how it could be done successfully.

Crosetti even went into the apparently minor detail of explaining that it was wise to change my bat every so often, since a player sours on one stick if he stays with it too long.

I'd been a fairly good hitter in the minors and I had every confidence that once I shook off the rookie shakes I could be the same with the Yankees. I certainly didn't think I'd have to change my batting style, but I did. McCarthy proved it to me. I always stood in the batter's box the same way, with my feet in the same spot whether I was facing a left-handed pitcher or a right-hander. It made no difference, I figured, if the pitcher was the type who threw tight or on the outside.

It takes pitchers a while to get hep to a batter's ways, just as the batter must study a pitcher before knowing what he throws, so I suppose I was as much a puzzle to them as they were to me the first two or three months. Later in the season, however, I found that everything I hit was on the handle of the bat. My thumbs felt as if they were breaking. The sting you get from the bat when the ball is hit on the handle is like an electric shock. It leaves your hands numb.

One day—and I recall it vividly because it was the only secret morning practice called after the season was on—I was hitting when McCarthy came up to me and asked, "How do you shift your feet?"

"I guess I don't shift them," I told him, realizing the storm was about to break over my head. Did he get mad! But any time McCarthy gets mad, you'll benefit. I shifted my feet thereafter.

McCarthy taught me how different pitchers operate and how hitters must change their styles with each. There was Ken

Chase, the Senators' left-hander, for instance, who was giving me so much trouble. Chase throws a curve in close that breaks on the handle of your bat. The rest of the fellows were killing him, but I couldn't get a loud foul.

Then, among others, there was the old master himself, Ted Lyons, of the White Sox, and Dutch Leonard, of the Senators, both knuckleball pitchers. Lyons can put that ball under your chin any time he wants. Now, with both, McCarthy pointed out, their knucklers break in such a fashion that a batter must stand up in front of the plate as much as possible. And I hadn't thought of shifting my feet or my position in the batter's box for any pitcher.

The same idea held true for Bob Feller, whose fast ball hops and whose curve breaks down. If I stood anywhere in the box but up front, I couldn't hit Feller with an oar. You're certain to hit under the ball and raise a lazy, easy foul or fan completely if you're not up enough in the box.

I remember thinking that Gerry Priddy was stretching a point when he'd put on what seemed to me an overdone act when we both played at Kansas City.

A favorite act of Gerry's in going after high flies that seemed certain to drop between infield and outfield was to run back and look first at the ball and then at the runner, one after the other, and shout and wave his arms as if signaling for the catch. I saw many a time when Gerry's gyrations left the opponent's coach unconvinced that the ball would fall safely and made him hold up the runner rather than risk a double play.

"Your facial expression as you're going for a fly ball is important," Gerry often said to me. "Even the movement of your eyes when you're waiting to make a play at a base may cause a certain amount of indecision for a base runner and slow him up just enough to throw him out."

When we both came up to the Yankees, I saw Gordon, Rolfe, and Crosetti go through these same histrionics to fool the base runner.

During my first major league weeks I wound up with welts all over my thighs as the result of being hit by the base runner when I was the middle man in a double play. I don't blame the fellows who banged into me. My job is to make the play, and theirs is to break it up by delaying or harassing the thrower. Despite the fact that at Kansas City in 1940 our club completed 193 double plays, a new record for the league, I obviously didn't know how to come into second base for the relay in more than one way. Truly, I didn't think there was more than one. Our major league opponents soon discovered this and made the most of it.

So Crosetti and Gordon, as well as McCarthy, stepped into the picture again. And showed me no less than three other ways to come in for the relay, get the throw away with all possible speed and avoid being hit.

(Gross pinch-hitting for Rizzuto: The lesson was well taught, for, with Rizzuto playing all but a month at shortstop, the Yankees in 1941 completed 196 double plays, a major league record that stood until last [1945] season. Rizzuto had a hand in 109 of them.)

I was feeling on the way up when the Yankees completed their first Western swing that season. Truth to tell, I hadn't been any ball of fire. After a good hitting start I fell off, but I figured I was just getting myself straightened out. On May 15 I bounced a double into the left field stands and was certain of it.

The following morning I reported to the stadium at about 11:30, just as I had done every other day. I went out on the field to limber up when I noticed Art Fletcher, McCarthy's first assistant, come over to Gerry Priddy. Fletch told Gerry that McCarthy wanted to see him. The team hadn't been going too well, as we all knew, but we figured we'd snap out of it. There didn't seem to be anything that a winning streak of three or four straight couldn't cure.

Priddy later returned to the dugout, and I could see he had to make an effort to keep from crying. My attention was taken from Gerry just then, however, when Fletch told me that Joe wanted to see me too. Before I left, Priddy came over and said, "I'm not playing today, Phil."

I told Gerry how sorry I was, but really didn't think I was due for the same medicine. Mr. McCarthy was sitting in his office just off the locker room when I entered.

After asking me to sit down, he said, "I'm going to give you a rest for a while, Phil."

I was benched too. The first time that had ever happened to me. It gave me more than that strange sinking feeling in the stomach bad news is supposed to bring.

"I wish you wouldn't take me out, Joe," I stammered, never realizing that that was probably the best thing that could have happened to me. When Crosetti was spiked just a month after I had been benched, I surely appreciated that stay on the bench.

"It will do you a lot of good to sit down for a while," Joe said quietly.

I doubted those words. I'd had my chance with the Yankees and had flopped. I was sure of it and certain that McCarthy was giving it to me by degrees and in a nice way. Both Gerry and I were through, I told myself. Later, when I was told that Rolfe, Gordon, and Crosetti had undergone the same ordeal — education by benching — I didn't want to believe it. I've found out how wrong I was since.

"You get a different view of the game, Phil, when you're sitting in the dugout watching your team and the other fellows out there," Joe tried to explain. "You've always viewed the game from the active player's angle; now view it from the other side and see what you can pick up. Keep on working out every day, just as you have, do a lot of running and fielding to keep your legs in shape, but when the game starts, I want you to sit near me. There'll be situations arising on the field I'll want to say something about. When they come up and I tell you something, just remember what you're told."

That very same day Joe started pointing out things during the game. I believe it was Dario Lodigiani, of the White Sox, who hit an unreachable blooper back of second. There was a man on first and he held up until it was certain the ball would drop safely. He reached second and started for third. Gordon retrieved the ball, took in the situation and instead of throwing to third ran back to the infield, his arm poised for a throw, but hanging onto the ball. Lodigiani was aching for an extra base, but couldn't break when Gordon refused to make a play at third. His quick eye had told him the odds against such a play were too long to justify the risk.

McCarthy reached over and tapped my knee, still keeping his eyes on the field. "There'll be times when you think a throw is called for. It would seem the natural thing to do. But sometimes the wiser move is to withhold the throw. Remember, don't give up an extra base when you don't have to."

All through that month my instruction continued. Watching the games from the bench, I got to see more and more how McCarthy wanted Yankees to play. Sometimes I was sure I'd have a situation figured, only to discover I hadn't.

There was the time the opposing pitcher was wild. I shouted to our hitters, "Make him pitch to you!"

"Why?" Joe asked. "The fellow's wild. He's having a tough time getting it over and he's got to ease up to get it in. It's a perfect spot to hit on the first pitch. It'll probably be a cripple that he figures he can sneak across."

Tommy Henrich was at bat one day against the (Philadelphia) A's. The situation appeared to call for a bunt, and I so expressed myself, though not to anybody in particular. There was a runner on third, and when Tommy took a low pitch I said, "Why doesn't he bunt the run in?"

Wrong again, Rizzuto.

"Don't second-guess," McCarthy cautioned. "There were plenty of times when you were at bat when the play called for a bunt and you tried to hit away."

The impression among most fans is that a player doesn't bunt unless he gets a signal from the coaching box. In certain cases, such as on a sacrifice play, that's true. But most times you're on your own, appraising the situation and laying it down if you think there is a fair chance of getting on base.

When I was leadoff man, a bunt seemed in order at many times. Later in the year, however, when I shifted to the eighth slot, I had to be careful about laying one down. With the pitcher coming up next, it isn't exactly wise, since it might set up a double play.

A young player stepping in with the Yankees receives every advantage that a great organization can offer. I learned fully what it means to be a Yankee in one game against the Red Sox. Lefty Grove was pitching and I can truthfully say he was the most difficult pitcher I faced all last year. I don't believe I collected one safe hit off him.

It was during the month I was on the bench, but McCarthy sent me in as a pinch hitter. The screen wasn't up in center field, which made for a poor background for hitting. Grove threw me three pitches. I swung at the first and missed. I took the second, a perfect strike. I swung at the third, missed, and trailed my bat back to the bench.

McCarthy said nothing to me as I took my seat. Others had struck out against Grove before me. I felt, however, I had to say something. "I couldn't see the ball," I grumbled, pointing to the white background brought on by the absence of the screen.

McCarthy continued to look out over the field, but out of the side of his mouth, he said in a voice barely audible, "The rest do."

Blush? What do *you* think?

"There was a hard line drive into the seats, one of those screaming line drives. Nobody got hurt. Everybody got out of the way. But Phil said, on the air,' Holy cow, it's a wonder more people don't get killed coming to the ballpark.' All of us in the PR department almost passed out when he said that."

—*Marty Appel, former Yankee PR director, former executive producer of Yankee broadcasts for WPIX-TV*

── ■ **6** ■ ──

War Beckons

During the World Series of 1941, the war in Europe and elsewhere was in a full rage. Pearl Harbor and direct U.S. involvement was still months away, but most ball players, like most Americans, realized that it was just a matter of time before they were forced to get involved. Even Phil Rizzuto, who had been granted special status exempting him from service would soon be called on to serve his country.

On December 7, 1941, the United States would no longer be on the sidelines watching the war. It would become the newest participant after the bombing of Pearl Harbor stunned the United States that fateful Sunday morning. However, the draft—and the war for that matter—were the last things on Rizzuto's mind the night the Yankees clinched the World Series. It was party time for Rizzuto and the Yankees. For Phil, it was his first World Series celebration and he couldn't wait. But Phil never made it to the party. In the hours after the October 6 win, Phil Rizzuto's life took a dramatic turn—call it fate. Up to that evening, there had been few girlfriends for Phil. Certainly nothing serious. But that all changed the night of October 6, 1941.

Growing up, the shy baseball player was more interested in playing ball than being with girls. It wasn't until 1939, when he was in Kansas City, that he became involved with a young lady named Betty Dresser, according to Joe Trimble in the book, *Phil Rizzutto*. It wasn't particularly serious, said Trimble, but it was Phil's first true girlfriend. The relationship ended in tragedy when Betty died from a throat infection after she had a seemingly ordinary tonsillectomy after the 1940 season. Trimble wrote, "Mrs. Dresser, heartbroken, buried her (daughter) and erected a tombstone which she knew would have pleased her little girl. On it was carved a facsimile of a ball player which looks a great deal like Phil himself."

After the final game of the World Series, Trimble related how Joe DiMaggio asked his young friend for a ride to La Guardia Airport. He said he had to get back to San Francisco right away on business. Because of his pressing business on the west coast, Joe D would not make it to the team's victory party at the Hotel Commodore. Rizzuto agreed to take his childhood hero to the airport. He figured there'd be plenty of time to get back to the city for the party.

But Phil never made it to the Hotel Commodore where the Yankees were gathering. He ended up in Newark, New Jersey of all places, light years from New York City as far as Rizzuto was concerned. DiMaggio, as it happened, was scheduled to be the featured speaker at the Fireman's Annual Smoker in the Essex House Hotel in Newark. DiMaggio, who wasn't terribly upset about missing the team's victory party, felt bad that he couldn't keep his speaking engagement, which was set up by a friend of his. He asked Rizzuto to phone Newark Fire Chief Emil Esselborn, the head of the affair, with the bad news.

Rizzuto did as he was told after dropping off the Yankee Clipper. Esselborn persuaded Rizzuto to fill in. Scooter was hesitant, but finally agreed to come. He entertained the guests with baseball tales and also signed autographs. Later, Esselborn invited Phil to his home. Rizzuto accepted and as soon as he entered the Esselborn house and saw the chief's beautiful blonde daughter, Cora, he fell in love.

"I saw The Kid," Rizzuto said in Trimble's book, "and I

guess my eyes must have popped. I knew this was it. I went there for a cup of coffee and I was in love before I even got into the dining room. That was all. I didn't go home for a month!"

Indeed, Rizzuto was on fire. He courted Cora in person, on the phone, and spent just about every available minute with her. "I was walking on air when I left her at midnight (that first night)," Rizzuto continued. "I wanted to be with her all the time. I drove over to the Douglas Hotel in Newark and took a room. For 30 days straight we had dates. And after I took her home each night, I rushed back to the hotel and called her up. Then we'd talk for three hours more!" It mattered little that Cora was not a baseball fan. Phil had found the right girl.

He asked her to marry him in November. She declined. That didn't stop Rizzuto, though. After a brief trip out of town to lick his wounds over the rejection, he was back again and continued to see Cora. By then, however, the world was in turmoil. On December 7, the Japanese bombed Pearl Harbor and the United States announced its intention to join the war. The following summer of 1942 would become a rough one for Phil, not only because he could not see Cora as much as he wanted, but because he knew it was only a matter of time before he'd be joining so many other ball players in the war drive. Eventually, more than 300 players from 1941 major league rosters were to join one of the armed services.

With his peacetime classification outdated, Rizzuto would ultimately enlist in the Navy in August of 1942. He was able to hold up his report date and it was mutually decided between Rizzuto and his draft board that he would report to Norfolk, Virginia, on October 7, a couple of days after, they presumed, the Yankees would win the World Series.

Even with the distraction of falling in love and preparing to embark on a military career, Rizzuto, now earning $7,500, had an excellent sophomore season. He batted a solid .284, scoring 79 runs, driving in 68, and stealing a career-high 22 bases. It was also a great year afield, as well, as Rizzuto led American League shortstops in putouts with 324. Rizzuto accomplished all of this even though he suffered a mild concussion midway through the campaign after being accidentally kicked in the head by former Kansas City Blues teammate Billy Hitchcock. Rizzuto didn't think anything of it and played on, despite suffering from headaches and blurred vision. It wasn't until weeks later, after getting a checkup, that he discovered that he had suffered a concussion. By then, of course, he was practically fine.

All this came on the heels of Rizzuto being named to the American League All-Star team. Lou Boudreau was the junior circuit's starting shortstop on a team that featured a starting lineup of Boudreau, Tommy Henrich, Ted Williams, Joe DiMaggio, Rudy York, Joe Gordon, Ken Keltner, and Buddy Rosar. Among the reserves were Bobby Doerr, Birdie Tebbetts, Dom DiMaggio, and Rizzuto. For the National League, stars included Pete Reiser, Johnny Mize, Mickey Owen, and Mel Ott. Pee Wee Reese was among the National League reserves. On the field at the Polo Grounds, home of the New York Giants, the American League defeated the Nationals, 3-1, on first-inning homers by Boudreau and York. Rizzuto, hitting .235 at the break, did not see action in the game. Neither did most of the other American League reserves, as the winners used only one pinch-hitter in the contest.

The All-Star Game over, it was back to the regular season, where the Yankees were beginning to take command of the race. At the All-Star break, they led Boston by four games and Cleveland by seven. The lead grew dramatically. Ten days after "Pride of the Yankees," starring Gary Cooper, opened at the Astor Theater July 15 to patrons paying anywhere from 35 cents to $1.10, the Yankees were 13 games in front of both Cleveland and Boston. Lou Gehrig would have been proud.

At the same time, the war was raging. In the Pacific on July 26 the United States sunk five Japanese ships. Elsewhere, the Russians were being pushed back by the Nazis. Life in the major leagues went on, however, with President Franklin D. Roosevelt giving America's pastime the go-ahead back in January after consideration was given to halting the season. "I honestly feel it would be best for the country to keep baseball going," he said. "These players are a definite recreational asset to their fellow citizens, and that, in my judgment, is thoroughly worthwhile."

On August 14, Rizzuto was in on a major-league tying record of seven double plays as New York whipped the Athletics, 11-2. Rizzuto and second baseman Joe Gordon's exploits were described in the *New York Times* as the "scintillating keystone combination of Phil Rizzuto and Joe Gordon who at times moved so swiftly it was difficult for the eye to follow their lightning gyrations."

The Yankees, meanwhile, coasted to a second consecutive league title, finishing nine games ahead of Boston. Rizzuto went out and had a terrific World Series to give the fans a lasting impression before he departed for the Navy. The Scooter hit .381, cracking eight hits in 21 at-bats. It was far from enough, though, as the St. Louis Cardinals stunned the Yankees, 4 games to 1.

The Cardinals won 106 ball games that summer, taking the pennant by two games over Brooklyn, with Enos Slaughter, Marty Marion, and a young Stan Musial among the stars for the National League club. Still, the Yankees expected to quickly dispatch the Cards and go their separate ways. The Yankees won the first game, 7-4, as Red Ruffing outpitched Mort Cooper in St. Louis and it looked, indeed, as if they would be coasting to another world championship. But the Cardinals nipped New York, 4-3, in the second game, erasing a monster three-run homer by Charlie Keller in the eighth inning that tied the game. Ernie White hurled a six-hitter in the third game to shut down the Yankees, 2-0. It was the first time since 1926 —when the Yankees played St. Louis — that New York had been shut out in a World Series game. St. Louis took the fourth and fifth games by scores of 9-6 and 4-2. Keller slugged another homer in the fourth game, and Rizzuto banged one in the fifth off winning pitcher Johnny Beazley (who also won the second game). But overall, the pitching of St. Louis was too much for New York.

Ironically, the last time the Yankees had not won a championship after getting to the World Series was in 1926, to these same St. Louis Cardinals. The Yankees were without the services of Tommy Henrich for the series. The outfielder had left the team a month before for the Coast Guard. Had the Yankees won another game, they also would have been without the services of Rizzuto. Rizzuto, remember, was due in Norfolk October 7, whether or not the World Series was over. When they picked that date, Rizzuto and his recruiter both figured that the series would have been over in four or five games, with the Yankees, naturally, winning. When the series had ended, Phil never imagined that three seasons would go by before he'd wear Yankee pinstripes again.

Late in the 1942 season, with his service days nearing, Phil once again asked Cora to marry him, and this time, she agreed. No date was set, but Phil was ecstatic just the same. And so, Phil bid Cora a sad goodbye in October and left to join the Navy. While Cora was back home in Newark, New Jersey, with her parents, at least Phil could bide his time by enjoying the camaraderie of the many former ball players who were also wearing Navy blue. Players like Dom DiMaggio, Hugh Casey, Eddie Robinson, Pee Wee Reese, Bob Feller, and Freddy Hutchinson were at the Norfolk facility with Phil. In late January, Phil learned that his former double-play partner, Gerry Priddy, had been shipped along with Milo Candini to the Washington Senators for pitcher Bill Zuber and cash.

Priddy, who eventually played for four teams, never came close to reaching the stardom that was predicted for him. In 11 years, he batted .265 with 61 home runs. After 1942, he never again played in a World Series, although he did have a handful of quality seasons with the St. Louis Browns and Detroit Tigers. The news of Priddy, and other bits of news from back home, kept him going as he longed for Cora.

As the months passed, Phil's love for Cora had only grown, and he wanted to marry her as soon as possible. They finally agreed on a June wedding date. In the meantime, Rizzuto played a lot of baseball, sometimes seven days a week. The Navy players often played against each other, and against other teams. The biggest rivalry was between the Naval Training Station and the Air Station, and those games got pretty hot as they sought camp bragging rights. Many of the contests drew hundreds of spectators, often betting huge sums of money on the games.

On June 23, 1943, Phil and Cora were finally married. Naturally, the Scooter was wearing his Navy uniform for the ceremony at a small church near the base. His family and hers, as well as many of his baseball friends, were on hand. Afterwards, the couple enjoyed a party at the Monticello Hotel in Norfolk, and from there, Cora and Phil went on their "honeymoon." It wasn't much of a honeymoon, really, as they booked a suite at the Cavalier Hotel down the road. Ball players being ball players, of course, the honeymoon took a while to kick in because several of the players, according to Joe Trimble, infiltrated the newlyweds' room and sat down for a long game of hearts! A couple of hours later, the game over, the Rizzutos spent their first night together.

Fifty years later, Cora and Phil are still madly in love. As part of their 50th anniversary celebration, the Yankees planned a day for Cora and Phil in June 1993.

Shortly after they were married, Phil and Cora moved to a small apartment off base. Phil could live off base because he owned a car. Sort of. He owned a 1929 Model-A Ford, picked up when one of his soldier friends got shipped out. While it wasn't much of a car, it helped the Rizzutos get around town. It also proved to be the butt of many jokes, noted Trimble. On several occasions, players would steal the keys, and Phil would find the car in strange places, like the baseball field's wide-open dugout, or upside down. Bob Johnson of the Washington Senators reportedly peeled the roof off the car during one wild afternoon. It may have been Phil's car, but it was everyone else's toy.

The Rizzutos lived happily together in Norfolk for barely six months. At the end of 1943, the ball players were being shipped out, in response, in part, to complaints from government officials about what was perceived as preferential treatment. Rizzuto was sent to relatively quiet Gammadodo, New Guinea, a few days after New Year's Day. Naturally, he was heartbroken to leave his bride. Rizzuto understood the war situation, however, and realized that there was nothing he or Cora could do. He had barely settled in at his new base when he came down with malaria and was sent to a hospital in Brisbane, Australia, for treatment.

Shortly thereafter, Cora, now back with her parents in Newark, gave birth to the couple's first child, Patricia Ann, on March 8, 1944. Thousands of miles away, Rizzuto, now recovered from his bout with malaria (although he would have after-effects for years afterward), would soon get new orders to report to Hawaii. Not to fight, but to play baseball. As a means of building morale among the troops overseas, the services decided to have an Army-Navy series. Both squads were chock-full of outstanding ball players, including Rizzuto, Joe Gordon, Johnny Mize, Virgil Trucks, Joe DiMaggio, Schoolboy Rowe, Johnny VanderMeer, and Pee Wee Reese. Bill Dickey was the manager of the Navy team and had to decide between Reese and Rizzuto at short. Dickey went with Reese.

"I don't think it was because I was a better shortstop than Phil," offers Reese. "Maybe they thought Phil could play third base better than me. I don't know. Maybe it was because I had been playing there for a while and Phil was flown in. We didn't think anything about it. I know I didn't, and I'm sure Phil didn't either."

The Navy ended up dominating the heavily attended series, winning five of seven games at Honolulu Stadium. The series over, Rizzuto was shipped back to New Guinea, and in January 1945, to the Philippines. Here, Rizzuto, now a specialist, first class, was assigned to the SS *Triangulum* and oversaw a four-man gun crew. He told Trimble, "We took a few pot shots at Jap planes that were snooping around now and then, but never hit one." That would be Rizzuto's only "battle" action during the war. In the coming months, Rizzuto attained his highest level in the Navy, that of chief petty officer. In August, of course, the Japanese surrendered, after the atomic attacks on Hiroshima and Nagasaki. In September, Rizzuto was on a ship bound for the United States, and on October 28, he was released from the Navy.

The Associated Press moved this short story over the wire:

"Norfolk, Virginia, Oct. 28 (AP) — Phil Rizzuto, former shortstop of the New York Yankees, was discharged from the Navy today. Rizzuto, an athletic specialist, enlisted following the 1942 World Series between the Yankees and Cardinals. The little infielder who served in Australia and the Philippines for 19 months, left for his New York home tonight."

By the spring of 1946, Rizzuto was ready to roll. So were the Yankees, who were now being run by former Dodger executive Larry MacPhail, Dan Topping, and Del Webb, who bought out the late Colonel Jacob Ruppert's heirs in a $2.9 million deal. The Yankees, who finished first in 1943, had dropped to third in 1944 and fourth in 1945 and were eager to get back on track. In '43, New York easily outdistanced the Washington Senators to win the pennant and then defeated the St. Louis Cardinals in five games in a rematch of the World Series. This time, the Yankees had superior pitching. Spud Chandler, the American League Most Valuable Player, was the ace during the regular season with a 20-4 record (1.64 ERA) and won a pair of series games, including a 2-0 shutout in the clincher.

Frank Crosetti started the majority of games at shortstop that year (after serving a 30-day suspension at the beginning of the season for pushing an umpire during the 1942 World Series) and batted .233, with George "Snuffy" Stirnweiss also garnering time and hitting .219. In 1944, the Yankees fell to third, behind the St. Louis Browns and Detroit Tigers. Mike Milosevich became the team's first-string shortstop ahead of Crosetti, with Stirnweiss moving to second base. Milosevich played all of 1944 and part of

1945, and was out of the majors with a lackluster .241 career mark, as major league rosters began to fill up again with servicemen returning home.

The 1945 Yankees hit rock bottom as far as they were concerned, falling to fourth place and playing with a makeshift lineup that could not have beaten either of their two top farm clubs—Kansas City or the Newark Bears—before the war. Crosetti was again the team's No. 1 shortstop and hit .238.

Immediately looking to make up for lost time in 1946, on the field, and at the gate, MacPhail scheduled a series of preseason games in steamy hot Panama. The Panamanians loved Rizzuto, calling him "La Cucaracha," which translates to "the cockroach," because of his lightning-quick movements afield. During the opening weeks, however, Rizzuto got sick, apparently as an after-effect of his malaria. He wasn't doing very well, and late in the spring, there were stories circulating that he might be through.

A big deal was made with the signing of a kid out of UCLA, Bobby Brown, who would, years later, become the president of the American League. Brown, who grew up in New Jersey and attended Columbia High School in Maplewood, minutes away from Rizzuto's hometown of Hillside, would be sent down to the Newark Bears of the International League for further seasoning. Even if Brown was down on the farm, though, Rizzuto didn't feel terribly secure.

Picked to win the pennant, the Yankees struggled early in the season. Boston jumped out to a huge start and never really looked back. The Red Sox won 104 games that year under manager Joe Cronin, finishing ahead of second-place Detroit. New York, a distant third, was 17 games back. In May, reports that Joe McCarthy was not happy with the new regime, nor it with him, began to surface. At the end of the month, McCarthy was out of action with a cold for four days. On the fifth, the announcement came that he had resigned. The Yankee manager since 1931, McCarthy said in a letter to MacPhail, "It is with extreme regret that I must request that you accept my resignation as manager of the Yankees Baseball Club, effective immediately. My doctor advises that my health would be seriously jeopardized if I continued.

"This is the sole reason for my decision which, as you know, is entirely voluntary upon my part. I have enjoyed our pleasant relationship and I was hoping it would continue until we won a championship. I am going to miss the team very much and I am sure that they are going to continue on to win the pennant and the world championship."

And so, McCarthy was out and Bill Dickey was in. Rizzuto was saddened by McCarthy's departure but he had his own concerns as he continued to work his way into shape after his three-year layoff from major league competition. Things didn't get any better for the Bronx Bombers, though, even with the change in managers. It wasn't a good year for anybody. Even Joe DiMaggio — suffering from a bone spur in his left heel — could not do the job he was used to, batting just .290, a career low. He did club 25 homers and drive in 95 runs, but to "The Clipper," it was not the kind of season he expected of himself.

Rizzuto hit a low note on July 17 when he was hit by a pitch in his left temple in the second game of a doubleheader with St. Louis. Rizzuto collapsed to the ground as 30,159 Yankee Stadium fans sat hushed.

"Phil was carried on a stretcher from the field to the dressing room, where examination by Dr. Robert Emmet Walsh diagnosed the injury as a concussion. Ice packs were applied until an ambulance arrived to remove Rizzuto to New York Hospital," the *New York Times* reported.

Luckily for Rizzuto, who would later be the first American Leaguer to wear a helmet, it was not a serious injury. A few inches higher and it could have been quite a serious head injury. While other hitters might balk at batting following a beaning such as that, Rizzuto seemed to relish the opportunity. Batting a mere .222 at the time of the beaning, he sizzled in the weeks ahead. By the end of the season, he had gotten his average up to .257, not bad considering where he once was.

Ironically, as bad a season on the field as it was for the Yankees, the New York club drew over two million fans. Part of the reason for the huge attendance figures can be traced to the fact that the Yankees introduced night baseball to Yankee Stadium in May. Another reason is simply that baseball fans were thrilled to see "major league" ball again after watching predominantly reserves for three years.

MacPhail, who earlier had brought many innovations to the Dodgers, was reponsible for bringing the lights to the stadium. Also that year, he introduced air travel to the Yankees and, in fact, New York became the first major league team to travel exclusively by air. Many of the players, fearful of planes, complained about the new arrangement. Rizzuto was one of those players, and to this day, has a fear of flying.

It's hard to say how many of those two million fans would have reacted had their popular shortstop jumped to the Mexican League. But, it came pretty close to happening during the early part of May.

Jorge Pasquel, a wealthy Mexican, was intent on bringing a third major league into the fold down in Mexico. He, or his associates, approached dozens of major leaguers beginning in spring training. Rizzuto was one of the most sought-after ball players. As the season began and Rizzuto could not produce as he wanted, the big money being thrown at him by Pasquel and his people were staggering. At the time, he was making just $7,500 with the Yankees. He had heard that Mickey Owen of Brooklyn had already jumped, taking a $90,000 offer, and other notable stars were being lured. Not even the threat of being blackballed stopped Rizzuto from listening early on. The Scooter, perhaps thinking of the Bobby Brown signing that spring, was wondering if his days were numbered as a Yankee. In the end, Pasquel might have gotten the Yankee star, except that Pasquel's brother went a step too far.

Rizzuto related the tale to Dan Daniel of *The Sporting News*. In part, he said, "Was it serious? Man, I practically was right in the Mexican League, and if that Bernardo Pasquel had kept his trap shut, and had not announced that he had me signed up, while I was still in New York, I undoubtedly would have gone down there—against the much better judgment of Mrs. Rizzuto. I haven't often disputed that judgment since.

"You will recollect the 1946 season. Joe McCarthy quit on May 24, Bill Dickey took his place. Things were topsy-turvy. We finished third.

"I was worried to death, insecure, hounded and harassed by the fear that I was washing up. No foolin.'

"Well along comes this Bernardo Pasquel with an offer. He wanted to pay me $100,000 for three years, one-third deposited in a New York bank immediately.

"Pasquel wined and dined us at the Waldorf. He met me after games and urged me to grab the chance. I figured he was doing me a big favor. I was over 21 and well able to make my own decisions, and it was no case of a man from Mexico luring a green rookie off the right path," continued Rizzuto, who was 28 years old at the time.

"Bernardo said he would pay all expenses of moving us to Mexico City. He promised to pay our living expenses, in a fine apartment down there.

"Cora opposed the scheme. She said I would do better sticking with the Yankees. She protested about uprooting the family. She made me stop and think. But there was the hundred grand — and security.

"Bernardo said, 'Call McCarthy now, and tell him you are home in bed, with a bad cold. Then we will go down the street, buy a Cadillac, drive down to Mexico, and install you in the Mexican League. Once down in Mexico, you will call up McCarthy and tell him the truth.'"

That bothered Rizzuto, who was endeared to McCarthy, and he began to balk at the whole deal. Pasquel irked Rizzuto more by announcing publicly that the deal had been made. The Yankees immediately "went to court for an injunction, and asked me to sign the papers," Rizzuto continued, realizing that he was now in the driver's seat. Rizzuto told MacPhail that he really didn't want to go to Mexico, but it was a matter of dollars and cents. "MacPhail gave me a check for $5,000 and promised me a bonus if I would have a fairly good season. I did not have a good season, so I did not get the bonus. Yes sir, it was a close call. Imagine what would have happened if I had jumped to Mexico?" Rizzuto found out soon enough, as the league ran into financial troubles and didn't last very long.

When his teammates heard about the scam, they played countless pranks on the little guy. Of course, this was no different than with anything else. Rizzuto had his share of pranks played on him, whether it was in the minor leagues, major leagues, or in his post-baseball career in the booth.

"They played a lot of jokes on him," remembers Yogi Berra. "We used to leave our gloves on the field. They put cockroaches in there. Sometimes they'd put dirt in there. Phil was very scared, you know. I remember one time we were on a train and Johnny Lindell put a lobster in his bed."

Pete Suder, predominantly a second baseman with the Philadelphia Athletics over a 13-year career, constantly pulled pranks on Rizzuto. "In those days we used to leave our gloves on the field," acknowledges former Yankee outfielder Gene Woodling. "Pete Suder, if you remember that name, he was a son of a gun. God, he used to get toy snakes and all kinds of bugs and put them in Phil's glove. When Phil picked that glove up he was all over the place. Well, I tormented him that way, too. I did a few things. We had a lot of fun."

Although there is plenty of evidence to the contrary, Tommy Henrich insists that the Yankees were not the responsible party for Rizzuto pranks. "That's a bunch of hooey. The Yankees didn't do that to him. Kansas City did that to him. We weren't in that mold. Well, we had a couple of guys like big John Lindell. OK, he'd pull a prank on Phil. The old idea you left your glove on the field and somehow or another Lindell would put, say, a grasshopper or a frog in there."

In the spring of 1947, it was no joke as the Yankee brass wanted to start anew, and brought in another manager, Bucky

Harris, to lead the quest to regain the championship flag. A rookie, Yogi Berra, came to camp and was expected to aid the cause. Bobby Brown, who hit .341 at Triple-A Newark in 1946, would see time as well. In other moves, the Yankees picked up pitcher Allie Reynolds from Cleveland, with Joe Gordon heading to the Indians in one of those "maybe they'll do better in another setting" type trades. Gordon came back from the war and had suddenly become ineffective at the plate, batting just .210 in 1946, with only 11 home runs and 47 RBIs. Reynolds, meanwhile, was 11-15 with a 3.88 ERA for the Indians. Reynolds would respond wonderfully to the move, becoming the Yankees' top pitcher with a record of 19-8. Gordon clicked at Cleveland, as well, batting .272 with 29 home runs and 93 RBIs, the latter two statistics club highs.

Berra, who remains good friends with Rizzuto today, roomed with him briefly in 1947 and recalls good times. "We played a lot of cards on the train. We used to go to the movies. We had a lot of fun. But I guess I stayed up too late for him. He didn't want to room with me for very long."

The season didn't start particularly well, when Joe DiMaggio, hampered by the after-effects of bone-spur surgery, was sidelined during spring training. But he came back four games into the season and the Yankees caught fire almost immediately. They won 19 games in a row beginning in late June, and when the streak was over, had taken a substantial lead in the standings. When the season had ended, the Yanks were 12 games ahead of Detroit and raising the American League flag at the stadium, their first in four years, as over two million fans passed through the turnstiles. In April, 60,000 fans packed the ballpark for "Babe Ruth Day" and 74,747 jammed the stadium for a night game in May. The Yankees also featured their first "Old Timers Day," now a tradition at Yankee Stadium and other ballparks. DiMaggio won the Most Valuable Player award, and Phil Rizzuto was back. The Scooter hit .273, driving in 60 runs, and made just 25 errors in 153 games.

In the World Series that year, the Yankees faced the Dodgers in a rematch of the 1941 series, but with more intensity. The arguing began during the spring when Brooklyn coach Charlie Dressen moved to the Yankees. Dodger general manager Branch Rickey and manager Leo Durocher were furious and charged that Yankee executive Larry MacPhail, who used to work for the Dodgers, had entertained gamblers at an exhibition game in Havana, Cuba, during spring training.

MacPhail denied the charges and countered with a suit against Durocher. Durocher kept at it through Harold Parrott of the *Brooklyn Eagle*, blasting the Yankees repeatedly in print. Happy Chandler, the commissioner of baseball, finally got involved and when the dust had cleared, suspended Durocher for the 1947 season for his part; Parrott was fined $5,000, Dressen was suspended for 30 days, and the Yankees and Dodgers were both leveled fines of $2,000. Clyde Sukeforth ran the team briefly, then Burt Shotton took over and the Dodgers responded by winning the pennant by five games over St. Louis.

It was quite a year for Brooklyn, which was joined by Jackie Robinson, the first black ball player to play in the major leagues. The Cleveland Indians and the St. Louis Browns brought aboard Larry Doby and Hank Thompson, respectively, later in the year. Ironically, Thompson would become the New York Giants' first black player in 1949. The Yankees, by the way, were one of the last major league teams to have a black on their roster. It wasn't until 1955, when New York brought up Elston Howard, that the Yankees broke the color line.

The only clubs to add black players after that were the Philadelphia Phillies (1957), the Detroit Tigers (1958), and the Boston Red Sox (1959). Robinson had a superb year, hitting .297 with 12 homers despite receiving a less-than-warm welcome from around the league. Pee Wee Reese batted .284 and also whacked 12 homers. In addition, excellent seasons were put in by Dixie Walker, Carl Furillo, Pete Reiser, and Ralph Branca, who won 21 games.

It was a classic World Series, shown on network television (NBC) for the first time (television was still very new; few people had TV sets), and it went down to the wire. The Yankees won the opener, 5-3, when they exploded for five runs in the fifth inning after Brooklyn starter Ralph Branca had retired the first 12 batters he faced. New York won the second game, as well, behind the pitching of Allie Reynolds and a 15-hit attack, 10-3.

With the series moving to Ebbetts Field, the Dodgers came back to win Games 3 and 4, 9-8 and 3-2. To this day, the most memorable game of the series was the fourth. With two out in the ninth inning, Cookie Lavagetto smacked a double with two on to end a no-hit bid by Bill Bevens. The double scored both runs, giving Brooklyn a one-run win.

The Yankees finally won a game at Ebbetts on October 4, nipping the Dodgers, 2-1, behind the clutch pitching of Spec Shea, who won his second game of the series. Brooklyn won Game 6, 8-6, at the stadium, but the Yankees clinched the series in Game 7, 5-2, as Joe Page picked up the victory in relief. Page had a terrific Series, pitching in relief in four games. Rizzuto did his part, too. He hit .308, and in the field had a perfect performance, setting a World Series mark for putouts by a shortstop with 18. He also had 15 assists.

In those days, ballplayers could not rely on their baseball salaries, even if they also got a World Series share. So during this period, Rizzuto got involved with a popular clothing store on Broad Street in Newark, the American Shops. The owner would bring in ball players to lift sales or just to attract attention to his store. Indeed, when the players were there, the store was crowded. Not all of the customers were looking to buy a fashionable zoot suit, either.

"Phil and I had a lot in common," says Gene Hermanski, who played with the Brooklyn Dodgers. "We're both from Jersey. We lived within a couple of miles of each other. I lived in Irvington at the time, and he lived in Hillside, where he still lives. We were almost neighbors. In fact, we worked together off-season at a men's store in Newark many, many years. The American Shops. This guy that owned it was a promoter. He figured that by getting ball players in, it would be like advertising. We'd go in on Wednesdays and Saturdays and people would flock in. The guy was right. The place would be mobbed. I remember Joe D came down once or twice, Yogi Berra, Ralph Branca, Bobby Thomson, Jerry Coleman, they all came down. So did others, I believe. He would rotate us and the guy made millions of dollars." Rizzuto enjoyed the job, which was good for a few extra bucks, and even considered getting into the clothing business upon his retirement.

Meanwhile, just as quickly as the Yankees had regained their elite level in 1947, they plummeted in 1948. The Yankees were beset by front office dissension (Harris was dimissed a day after the season ended), and the team was plagued by injuries. Rizzuto suffered a tear in his right thigh early in the season, and the leg never really healed, forcing him out of the lineup for 13 games in May. He somehow played the majority of the rest of the campaign. In addition to his bad leg, his eyes bothered him, and of greater concern, his throwing arm caused him problems. DiMaggio had problems, too, and after the season, he had surgery to remove a bone spur in his *right* heel. Rizzuto managed to avoid surgery, opting, with the team's okay, to give it plenty of rest instead.

The Yankees finished in third place, behind Cleveland and Boston, and Rizzuto finished the way he started — struggling. He batted a career-low .252. If there was one saving grace it was that he had his best fielding season yet, making just 17 errors. However, with the bad arm, he was unable to make many of the plays he normally would have. Strangely, Rizzuto was given a "day" by the fans on August 29. It was probably Rizzuto's most memorable day of the season in a year when little went right for Rizzuto or the Yankees.

The Yankees' demise that year wasn't the only sad note. On June 13, the Yankees, knowing that the "Bambino" had little time left, again honored Ruth. Ruth, who had his Number 3 retired that day, gave his farewell speech, and two months later he was dead. Rizzuto was among the 100,000 people who paid their last respects to Ruth as he lay in state at the "House that Ruth Built."

Any way you looked at it, 1948 was not a memorable season for Phil Rizzuto or the New York Yankees. Who would have ever known that the greatest championship run was about to begin?

"It was spring training one year and we're televising the first game back to New York. I was assigned to interview Steinbrenner and Phil was assigned to interview Billy Martin. I finished mine and we went to a break and while we were waiting for Phil to interview Billy, Billy pulls a rubber snake out of his pocket and puts his hand around Phil and leaves the snake there (on his shoulder). Just as the red light was going to go on, Phil looked up and saw the snake and starts running toward center field. But he was all hooked and the lines caught him and pulled him back."

—*Bill White*

7

Five in a Row

Yankee management did not sit still during the off-season after the 1948 campaign. With Harris gone, 58-year-old Casey Stengel was brought in to lift the fortunes of the New York Yankees. On the surface, it was a strange move. Stengel had not been very successful in his previous major league experiences, failing to bring winners to either the Brooklyn Dodgers or the Boston Braves. But after a splendid run with Oakland of the mighty Pacific Coast League, it was he who got the nod. Little did Yankee management realize that the man it had hired would soon lead the club to five straight world championships. At the time, they were only concerned about 1949.

One of Stengel's first pieces of business had to do with Rizzuto and his weak arm. There was concern among the brass, and Stengel was told to keep a close eye on Rizzuto's wing. He needn't have worried. During the winter, Rizzuto was careful not to overextend himself, and by spring training, he was feeling pretty good.

"The arm was tired," Rizzuto said in a *Sporting News* article after the 1949 season. "All it needed was rest. I spent the offseason doing nothing. Just that job I had in a Newark men's shop, plugging clothes. I did not have to throw anybody out."

Still, Stengel told Rizzuto during the spring of 1949 to take his time getting ready. Although the new manager was considering options should Rizzuto's career be through, he was well aware that a healthy Scooter was the preferred choice. Phil played in a handful of exhibitions, but it wasn't until the spring schedule was nearly over that Rizzuto put himself in full time. By April 1, he was sure he was ready. Joe DiMaggio was not. After undergoing surgery the previous November for the removal of the bone spur on his right heel, the Yankee Clipper never quite healed properly. He had a tough time running the bases that spring. Finally, he was flown to Johns Hopkins University in Baltimore, Maryland, for another operation, which would keep DiMaggio out for nearly half a season.

Rizzuto, however, was on fire as the year started. He batted close to .300 throughout the early months and helped keep the Yankees at the top of the standings even with a pulled muscle (suffered during a spring training game in Texas before the team headed north) hampering his play somewhat during the first six weeks. "The solid man of our club is Rizzuto," outfielder Tommy Henrich told Dan Daniel of *The Sporting News* after injuring his back, becoming what would be one of over 70 injury or illness victims for the Yankees that summer. "Just so long as Phil is at short, don't worry. If our injury hex should get him, too, you can scratch us off the list."

Rizzuto nearly became a victim of the injury hex late in June. It happened on June 28, ironically, during a big three-game series with the Joe McCarthy-managed Boston Red Sox (McCarthy replaced Joe Cronin after the 1947 season) that marked the return of DiMaggio. DiMaggio would return in lightning fashion, smashing four homers and driving in nine runs, as the Yankees swept the series.

The Yankees—who were out of first place just four days during the entire year—had started the season well ahead of everyone else, built a huge lead, and now the Red Sox were threatening to make their move. No matter what the standings, though, this rivalry is a heated one to this day. In 1949, with hot Boston in pursuit of New York, this series had all the makings of a heart-stopper. Both clubs were prepared to fight hard—and they did.

Playing before a packed house in the series opener at Fenway Park the evening of June 28, the fireworks began in the very first inning when Johnny Pesky slammed into Rizzuto during a force play at second base. Rizzuto was sent over on his head. The *New York Times* reported that "Rizzuto and Pesky collided while the Scooter was making a double play in the first. It appeared that Rizzuto was hurt, but after a couple of minutes he arose and continued in the game." But after the game, which featured several other rough incidents, Rizzuto complained of a headache.

DiMaggio couldn't have felt any better. In his first at-bat, he cracked a single over the left side of the infield and later scored on Hank Bauer's three-run homer. In the third inning, Rizzuto led off with a single and scored moments later when DiMaggio belted a home run off of Mickey McDermott as the Yankee bench erupted. Allie Reynolds and Joe Page held off Boston as New York won, 5-4, before more than 36,000 fans.

Rizzuto played the next day, and even though he complained that he wasn't feeling well, made a couple of key fielding plays to secure a victory. At the plate, he whacked a pair of doubles, laid down a perfect squeeze bunt, and drove in two runs as he went 3-for-4. It was a wild game, with the Red Sox blowing an early 7-1 lead. In the fifth inning, DiMaggio crushed another home run, scoring both Rizzuto and Henrich, who had walked. DiMaggio capped the day with a home run in the eighth to break a 7-7 tie, as the Yankees won their second straight in Boston, this time 9-7.

Rizzuto may have been feeling shaky, but no one noticed. The *New York Times* pointed out, "Rizzuto, by the way, continues to field sensationally and contribute timely hits. He bobbed up with three gems today." In the first inning, it noted, "a freak double play saved the Yankees. With the bases filled, Kinder slammed a hot liner off Marshall's glove. The ball then hit second base, caromed off Coleman's glove and Rizzuto scooped it up. The Scooter stepped on the bag, and fired to Henrich for the twin killing."

The next morning, Rizzuto went for X-rays of his aching head, and they came up negative. His jaw was awfully sore, but other than that, nothing else seemed wrong. Until game time. In the first inning of the series' third game, Rizzuto suddenly developed a twitch in his right arm. He was rushed to the hospital after batting just once in the game

It was a busy day for Rizzuto on the medical front. The *New York Times* reported that "Phil Rizzuto had a double-date with the doctors today. This morning he had his head x-rayed because of pains and dizziness which followed Tuesday night's collision with Pesky. The results were negative. Suddenly, in the last half of the first, the Scooter developed a cramp in his right wrist and forearm. He immediately went to Massachusetts General Hospital to be examined by Dr. William Sweet, neurologist specialist."

Tests "disclosed no blood clot, and Dr. Sweet said Rizzuto's condition—he still had a tremor in his right arm—might be post-traumatic as a result of his collision with Pesky."

"They glued 24 wires to my hair, and began to listen to what was going on in my mind," Rizzuto told reporters the next morning. "They listened and listened, and they must have heard nothing, because the doctor told me he had heard no serious symptoms. The hardest part was washing the glue out of my hair."

Rizzuto was sent home and told to take it easy for a day or two to see how he felt. While Rizzuto was taking it easy, his teammates were feeling on top of the world as they swept the Sox. DiMaggio hit his fourth homer late in the game, and with Vic Raschi outpitching Mel Parnell, the Yankees won again, 6-3. When the dust had cleared, Boston had gone from third place (behind the Philadelphia Athletics) to fifth, eight games out of first place.

The classic Rizzuto swing. As an early teen (left), Rizzuto honed his batting swing on the sandlots of Brooklyn. In the major leagues (below), Rizzuto perfected the art of bunting.

Rizzuto's 1941 rookie season was highlighted by Joe DiMaggio's amazing 56-game hitting streak, Rizzuto's award as the league's top rookie, and a World Series victory over the Brooklyn Dodgers. Shown here with his 1941 World Championship teammates, Rizzuto is seated in the first row, second from the left.

Rizzuto and his baseball idol, Joe DiMaggio, strike a classic pose before a Yankee game.

Rizzuto spent the 1943-45 seasons in the United States Navy. On leave from the Navy, Phil and his wife, Cora, take in a ball game at Yankee Stadium.

Rizzuto (far left) joins Casey Stengel (holding the ball) and his teammates in celebrating the Yankees' 1949 World Series victory over the Brooklyn Dodgers.

As evidenced by his lifetime fielding average of .968, Rizzuto's talents always shined the brightest in the field — whether it was clowning around with teammates (right) or making a key play at second base (below).

New York Yankees

New York Yankees

Capping an incredible run of five straight World Series Championships, Rizzuto and Billy Martin (left) hug after the Yankees' 1953 World Series triumph over the Brooklyn Dodgers.

Rizzuto and his wife, Cora, proudly show off their three daughters: Penny, in Rizzuto's arms; Cindy, standing in front; and Patti. Phil Jr. came along on January 17, 1956.

National Baseball Library and Archive, Cooperstown, NY.

The Old Timers games at Yankee Stadium always bring out the legends of major league baseball. Shown here from left to right are Billy Martin, Joe DiMaggio, Mickey Mantle, Whitey Ford, and Phil Rizzuto.

New York Yankees

Before the 1992 Old Timers game, Rizzuto joked with former Yankee greats Hank Bauer (left) and Tommy Byrne (center). After the game, Rizzuto(below) admired the portrait of Babe Ruth that hangs in the Executive Lunchroom at Yankee Stadium.

New York Yankees

Rizzuto's favorite charitable event is the celebrity golf tournament he hosts each year with Ed Lucas to raise money for St. Joseph's School for the Blind. Rizzuto also served as matchmaker for Ed and his fiancée, Allison Pfiefle.

Although Rizzuto has not yet been inducted in the Hall of Fame, his glove (top right) and shoes are shown in a Yankee display at Cooperstown. Interestingly, however, Rizzuto claims that the glove on display is not his.

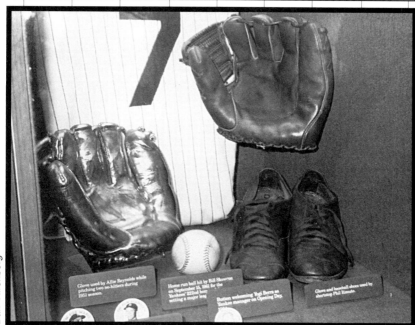

Rizzuto's "office" in the hall outside the WPIX broadcast booth is open to all fans who want to talk Yankee baseball.

Rizzuto and WPIX partner Tom Seaver (far right), are joined by former Yankee broadcaster George Grande (center), who now broadcasts for the St. Louis Cardinals.

As it turned out, Rizzuto felt fine by the next morning and was ready to play ball again. Rizzuto would miss one game, the only one he missed all year, and then was back in the line-up as the Yankees headed toward the All-Star break. As well as Rizzuto was playing, though, he could not muster enough support to make the All-Star team that summer. The fans voted for Eddie Joost of the A's to start, with Vern (Junior) Stephens of Boston finishing second. Lou Boudreau, the American League manager that year, opted to go with Stephens as the backup, keeping with the fans' desires. As it turned out, Joost batted just .263 that season, and Stephens went into a slump late in the year that may have helped cost the Red Sox the pennant.

Stephens may have slumped, but the Red Sox got hot as the summer wore on and the Yankees struggled. Boston was actually in a position to claim the pennant on the last weekend of the regular season. Trailing at one point by 12 games, Boston had bounced back. On the next-to-last weekend of the season, the Red Sox swept an unusual three-game series from the Yankees. It was unusual in that the first two games were in Boston, while the third was played in Yankee Stadium.

It was beginning to look as if New York would be disappointed again as Boston took over first place for the first time that season. Rizzuto — or should we say, his glove—played a role in one of the losses. Rizzuto, who used just two gloves his entire career, was playing shortstop during the series finale when a line drive by Dom DiMaggio went toward Rizzuto with two runners on and New York leading 6-3 in the eighth inning. But the ball seemed to go through Rizzuto's glove as he leaped high, and by the time the inning was over, Boston had taken the lead and was on its way to the top of the standings with a 7-6 victory.

A week later, the teams met again at Yankee Stadium for a season-ending, two-game series. Boston had a one-game lead and needed just one win to take the flag. But the Red Sox got none. With Yankee starter Allie Reynolds ineffective, relief pitcher Joe Page also lost his composure in the first game. With the bases full (as a result of Reynolds), he walked in two runs to give Boston a 4-0 lead. But he got himself together before there was any further damage and picked up the win with 6 2/3 innings of excellent work, allowing just one single the rest of the way. "I remember the first game Boston had a 4-0 lead in the sixth or seventh inning when (Red Sox catcher) Birdie Tebbetts said to me, 'We're going to drink champagne tonight, tomorrow we'll throw a rookie and you guys are going to have an early vacation,' Rizzuto recalled years later in the *New York Post*.

"Well, that really burned me and I went back to the dugout and told everyone. We ended up beating them 5-4. Next day we beat them 5-3 when Jerry Coleman got a big base hit." Tebbetts, for his part, claimed that he never made the statement. New York tied the game at 4-4, and in the eighth inning, Johnny Lindell (who already had two hits) drilled a home run down the line in left field for the game winner. Twenty-four hours later, with the bases full, Jerry Coleman's double scored everybody, and a 2-0 lead became 5-0. The Red Sox were not through, however, and scored three runs in the ninth inning, but Birdie Tebbetts, the tying run at the plate, fouled out to Tommy Henrich at first base for the final out.

In a way, the pennant was a surprise even to the Yankees, who were picked by a panel of sportswriters to finish second behind Boston. They overcame so many injuries, the most serious of which was to DiMaggio. Yet they endured, and pretty handily for much of the season. Vic Raschi was the team's top pitcher with 21 wins, but Allie Reynolds, Tommy Byrne, and Ed Lopat also had fine seasons (Reynolds won 17, and Byrne and Lopat each won 15). At the plate, Henrich and Berra combined for 44 homers and nearly 200 RBIs. DiMaggio, who missed half the season, amassed a .346 batting average and slugged 14 homers (67 RBIs). It was Rizzuto, though, who proved the most valuable Yankee. By far, it was his best season to date and proved without a doubt that he was among the league's elite. Even if he did slow down in the World Series.

With Boston out of the way, the Yankees set their sights on Brooklyn, which won the National League pennant by one game over the St. Louis Cardinals, who finished with the same record as the Yankees, 97-57. After such a dramatic finish to the regular season, the Yankees' five-game victory over Brooklyn seemed anticlimactic, even if it was between neighbors. Tommy Henrich's ninth-inning homer gave New York a 1-0 victory in the opener, as Reynolds scattered two hits. In Game 2, Preacher Roe handcuffed the Yankees on six hits, 1-0 (benefiting from a second-inning single by Gil Hodges to drive in Jackie Robinson), but after that, it was all New York in terms of victories. The Yankees scored three runs in the top of the ninth inning to break up a 1-1 tie in Game 3 when Johnny Mize and Jerry Coleman had key hits. The Dodgers countered with a pair in their half of the inning (on homers by Luis Olmo and Roy Campanella), but Joe Page, pitching in relief of Tommy Byrne, held off Brooklyn to gain the victory. Two three-run rallies sparked the Yankees to a 6-4 win in Game 4, and DiMaggio's solo homer helped New York rout Brooklyn, 10-6, in the series clincher.

It wasn't a great series for Phil, who collected just three singles in 18 at-bats. As a team, the Yankees didn't do much hitting, batting a paltry .226 for the series. Bobby Brown, with a .500 average, was the team's leading hitter. For the Dodgers, Pee Wee Reese had a good series, banging out six hits in 19 at-bats after batting .279 with 16 homers and 73 RBIs in the regular season. During the World Series, when the Reese-versus-Rizzuto argument raged, Phil went around wearing a pin with Reese's face on it. Typical Phil, taking a nontypical stand.

It was a splendid year for Rizzuto, clearly the Yankees' MVP. He led the Yankees in games played, at-bats, runs scored, total bases, stolen bases, doubles, and triples. He was also the league's top shortstop. Yet it wasn't good enough to win the league MVP. That went to Ted Williams of Boston, who had a sensational year. Rizzuto was second in the voting, ahead of Joe Page. Williams, who received 13 first-place votes to just five for Rizzuto (outpointing Rizzuto 273-175), hit .343, cracked 43 homers, and drove in 159 runs.

The New York Chapter of the Baseball Writers voted Rizzuto their "Player of the Year" in February 1950. It wasn't the league MVP, but it was something. The big one, though, was right around the corner. The shortstop, who many had thought was through just a couple years earlier, was about to have the greatest season of his career. The Yankees rewarded the little guy for his efforts after the 1949 season with a contract reported to be near $35,000, making him among the highest-paid Yankees.

Spring training in 1950 came soon enough and Rizzuto looked sharp during the preseason. Real sharp, especially to one starry-eyed rookie lefthanded pitcher. "I remember joining the club from Kansas City in 1950 and Phil was my shortstop," says Whitey Ford. "I was in a dream world with Phil playing short, Joe in center, Billy Martin and Jerry (Coleman) at second, and Bobby Brown, Tommy Henrich, and Yogi. They were all my idols and all of a sudden I'm playing with them. I had been a Yankee fan since I was eight years old and I remembered Phil in my earlier years when I was still playing sandlot baseball around Queens and Long Island. And then, I'm at spring training with him. I remember the players used to play a lot of practical jokes on him. They'd put fake dynamite in his car and when he starts the ignition it starts whistling and explodes. Nothing really happens, but it scares the daylights out of Phil. They teased him a lot. So did players from other teams. They'd always be putting bugs and wet chewing tobacco in his glove."

However, once the season started, Rizzuto suddenly went into a dry spell. With Tommy Henrich out of commission after his left knee went out on him, and DiMaggio in a slump himself, the Yankees got off to an inauspicious start. Rizzuto had been doing so well in spring training, he was totally baffled by his sudden lack of punch. Then, with the help of Johnny Mize, the hulking Yankee first baseman, Rizzuto was hot again, and hot he remained for the entire campaign. "I began to use Mize's bats, and found myself hitting more solidly, with greater distance," Rizzuto reported in a June 7, 1950, edition of *The Sporting News*.

The bat was a huge 34-ounce piece of lumber. "I do not have trouble coming around with the 34-ounce stick, and I like the solid, authoritative impact of the heavier bat against the ball. That's the whole story. I have discovered no great secret." Rizzuto continued, "In fact, the so-called secret is an old one. Here is the formula: First you have to keep in shape. Get plenty of sleep. Be with a club that pays you what you are worth. Eat reasonably, have some fun. Then, you have to marry the right girl."

With Mize's bat in hand, Rizzuto's average soared. A month and a half into the campaign, he was batting .355. On the team's first western swing, Rizzuto hit .441. On May 22, he broke the American League record for consecutive errorless games at shortstop. He topped Joost's 1949 mark of 42 in a row. It was a heck of a night for Rizzuto, who had to evade several "errant" pitches by Cleveland starter Mike Garcia. This, in retaliation for Rizzuto's heads-up play in the first inning, when he scored a run by barreling into catcher Ray Murray. It was the 5-6, 160-pound Rizzuto against the 6-3, 220-pound bruising catcher.

When the dust cleared, Rizzuto had scored, but lay heaving for air on the ground. Rizzuto, hitting a scintillating .365 at the time, proved to be a terror that day. In the *New York Times*, it was reported that when "he wasn't hitting the dirt at the plate to escape pitches that came perilously close to his head, Rizzuto was badgering Mike Garcia or hammering his successor, Steve Gromek, touching off two vital Yankee rallies and keeping alive a rousing four-run ninth with which the champions effectually stifled Tribe ambitions" leading to a 7-3 victory.

As the All-Star break neared, with New York battling the Detroit Tigers, Boston Red Sox, and Cleveland Indians for first, Yankee manager Casey Stengel was not about to let the fans forget Rizzuto this time. He campaigned often as the voting deadline got close. Joe Trimble, in his book, *Phil Rizzuto*, recalled Stengel's words during the push. "I've seen some great boys in the short field in my time. But none of them ever did anything Phil has not shown this year. In fact, I would call my boy 'Mr.

Shortstop' because I cannot conceive of a better showing by Reese, Marion or any other shortstop in the game. So he won't hit the long ball like Stephens or Joost. But show me anything else he can't do better. He's the fastest shortstop in the league, covers the most ground, is the most accurate thrower, and has the surest hands. He can go get a pop fly better than anybody. No shortstop alive can make as many 'impossible' plays as Rizzuto. And did you ever see a better man on the double play? The fans are nuts if they don't vote for Rizzuto. And tell 'em I said so!"

Rizzuto's errorless streak finally ended at 58 games (288 chances) June 8 when he overran a grounder by Detroit's Bob Swift. He made just 14 errors all season, leading the league's shortstops with a fielding percentage of .982 (on 767 chances). As his errorless streak was ending, so was his long-overdue wait as an All-Star starter. The fans responded to Rizzuto's year by making him the starting shortstop at the July 11, 1950, All-Star game at Comiskey Park in Chicago. Rizzuto was ripping the hide off the ball by then, hitting .324, with 63 runs scored, 19 doubles, four triples, two home runs, and 30 RBIs. Manager Casey Stengel made him the leadoff hitter.

The rest of the American League lineup included Larry Doby of Cleveland (CF), George Kell of Detroit (3B), Ted Williams of Boston (LF), Walt Dropo of Boston (1B), Hoot Evers of Detroit (RF), Yogi Berra of New York (C), and Bobby Doerr of Boston (2B). The Yankees' Vic Raschi was the starting pitcher. For the Nationals, it was Robin Roberts on the mound, with the starting lineup featuring the likes of Ralph Kiner, Stan Musial, Jackie Robinson, Enos "Country" Slaughter, Andy Pafko, and Roy Campanella. The game lasted 14 innings, with the Nationals pulling it out, 4-3, on a Red Schoendienst home run. The game was dramatic in that Ted Williams was knocked out of action after crashing into the left-field wall flagging down a Ralph Kiner drive. Rizzuto had a fine day, getting two hits in six at-bats. He played the whole game, made two put outs and had two assists in the field.

Rizzuto continued to hammer the ball after the All-Star break and so did Joe DiMaggio, who was having his last great season. On June 20, Joe D cracked his 2,000th hit and would go on to bat .301 with 32 homers and 122 RBIs. Rizzuto was at .321 on August 1. On the 6th, he may have had his best day of the year. With the Yankees going against Bob Lemon of Cleveland, Rizzuto went 4-for-4, pounding two doubles and a triple and driving in four runs as New York routed the Indians, 9-0, before 66,726 in Cleveland. In the first inning, Rizzuto got his 1,000th career hit, singling to start the game off. "I would pitch him the same way I pitched against Joe DiMaggio," Lemon recalls. "Very carefully. But you couldn't stay with any one thing with Rizzuto. You had to move it around and try and keep it down. You had to keep from letting the ball get up."

It was a particularly hot race that summer, with the Yankees, Tigers, Red Sox and Indians all battling for position. The Yankees went to Boston for a series in the early part of September. Always a heated rivalry anyway, it took on a new dimension that week when Rizzuto received a threatening letter. "It was 1950 —September 6," he recalled in an Associated Press article years later. "I got a letter threatening me, Hank Bauer, Yogi Berra and Johnny Mize. The letter said if I showed up in uniform against the Red Sox, I'd be shot. I turned the letter over to the FBI, and you know what Casey Stengel did? He gave me a different uniform and gave mine to Billy Martin. Can you imagine that? Guess Casey thought it'd be better if Billy got shot. I had an escort everywhere I went in Boston that trip." With the threat hanging over them, the Yankees lost, 11-2. Rizzuto, Berra, Bauer, and Mize all played. Bauer had three hits, Rizzuto one, and Berra and Mize were hitless. Martin, wearing Rizzuto's uniform, did not play.

The Yankees finally clinched the pennant on September 29 when the Tigers lost to Cleveland and were mathematically eliminated. The New Yorkers were in Boston and celebrated their victory in the shadows of Fenway Park. The Yankees, with superior pitching, went on to blitz the Philadelphia Phillies in four straight in the World Series. Phil had his second straight lackluster series, getting only two hits in 14 at-bats, but by then, it was only a matter of time before he received the MVP award.

"He had a great year," states Whitey Ford, who was 9-1 as a rookie and was cited by *The Sporting News* as the top rookie in major league baseball. "Oh, he had a good year," remembers Yogi Berra, who had a pretty good one himself and hit .322 with 28 homers and 124 RBIs. "He had an outstanding year," adds pitcher Allie Reynolds, a 16-game winner. "He did everything well that year." So did the surprising Yankees, who drew more than two million fans for the fifth straight year, as they beat out Red Rolfe's Detroit Tigers by three games.

On October 26, Rizzuto gained the top award in all of baseball. Philip Francis Rizzuto was the American League's Most Valuable Player — by a wide margin. The Scooter finished with 284 points (16 first-place votes) out of a maximum of 322, beating out the league's leading hitter, Billy Goodman of Boston, who got 180 points. Yogi Berra was third with 146 points, followed by George Kell of Detroit, Bob Lemon of Cleveland, Walt Dropo of Boston, Vic Raschi of New York, Larry Doby of Cleveland, Joe DiMaggio of New York, and Vic Wertz of Detroit.

"You win the MVP you must have done something right," says the Yankee leftfielder that season, Gene Woodling. "He had a heck of a year. That was a year where his bat really came on. I mean, people didn't realize what a good hitter he was. His defense was always good. You don't win the MVP unless you've had a good year."

Indeed, Rizzuto proved once and for all that he was much more than just a decent hitter who could bunt for a base hit. Clearly, it all came together for Phil in 1950.

"You know, I have won a lot of awards," Rizzuto said to Dan Daniel of *The Sporting News* after he was named the winner. "But this Most Valuable Player award sure topped them all. To think that a committee of 23 writers, representing all the eight cities in the American League, not only voted me the No. 1 guy, but gave it to me by so big a margin. Sure I had hoped to get the award. I thought I might have a chance. But the way it turned out — well, I have been walking on a cloud!"

The press honored Rizzuto in newspapers across the country for his great season. In a way, it was ironic since Rizzuto was never one to seek out publicity. In an era when players and newspapermen often hung out together, drinking and playing cards, Rizzuto kept to himself for the most part, preferring to keep pace only with himself and his family.

Meanwhile, the awards kept coming for Rizzuto that winter. The man who had already been cited as the "Best Dressed Athlete of 1950," the "Sports Father of the Year" (his dedication to his children was well known), and the "Most Popular Yankee" by the fans, picked up the first Hickock Award as the "Outstanding Pro Athlete of 1950." The Hickock Award was especially satisfying to Rizzuto since it encompassed athletes from other sports. In 1950, Ben Hogan was having a fine year in golf, jockeys Eddie Arcaro and William Boland were riding lots of winners in horse racing, Jim Konstanty, the National League MVP, was in the running for the Hickock, and so were hockey players Ted Lindsay and Chuck Raynor, and basketball stars George Mikan and Dick McGuire.

Publicist Murray Goodman, who was hired by the Hickock Company of Rochester, New York, to create the award, recalls the events leading up to the prestigious award being given to Rizzuto. "I was the originator. The Hickock people, who made belts and jewelry, wanted me to create an award for a middleweight championship belt. It was originally named for S. Rae Hickock, the founder of the company and a real sportsman. He has long since died. So anyway, we created a belt for the (world championship) fight between Jake LaMotta and Marcel Cerdan (at Briggs Stadium in Detroit, June 16, 1949), but then Nat Fleischer (of *Ring Magazine*) began squawking like hell because he was giving boxing belts away for years. Anyway, we promised Nat that this would be the only belt we would give. Well, LaMotta won the belt (by knockout) and the stipulation was you win it and defend it, but when you lost, you give it to the next guy. LaMotta lost his next fight (in December 1949 to Robert Villemain, 10-round decision) and refused to give it back. So the Hickock people, fed up with it all, said we're getting out of the boxing business and asked me to give the Hickock Award some more thought. So we created the Professional Athlete of the Year award. There was no such award, and to this day, ours is the only award of its kind strictly for professional athletes, male or female. (The Hickock Award, which remained a belt valued at $10,000, was given out from 1950 to 1976, and beginning this year, will be issued again under its new sponsor, the Tandy Corporation. According to Goodman, the belt was actually worth about $30,000, and the new belt, to be awarded in January 1994, will be worth close to $75,000.)

"We used to present the award at a charity dinner in Rochester. I remember the first year with Rizzuto. We all went up by train to Rochester, New York, a 12-hour ride. We went on the Empire Special. We sat up all night and played cards. Nobody slept. The Rizzuto thing was amazing. Everybody loved him. After our dinner he went up to Jamestown (New York), where he was presented with another award."

Yankee management, thrilled with Rizzuto's performance, gave him a substantial raise to $40,000, making him the fourth-highest-paid Yankee of all time, behind Babe Ruth, Joe DiMaggio, and Tommy Henrich.

Rizzuto had another good year in 1951, although hardly comparable to his 1950 exploits. He hit .274 and was still a sparkplug, as witnessed by his memorable squeeze bunt on September 17, in the thick of the pennant race with Cleveland. The Indians were in town.

The teams were tied for first, and after eight and a half innings, the game was tied, 1-1. "With the bases full and one out in the last half of the ninth inning," *The New York Times* reported "two of the Bombers' most skilled campaigners, Li'l Phil Rizzuto and Joe DiMaggio, turned in a brilliantly executed squeeze play. Li'l Phil bunted the ball. The Clipper, timing his spurt from third base perfectly, streaked over the plate. A bewildered and crestfallen Bob Lemon stood some ten feet away, the ball in his hand but too late to do anything about it." The run in, the Yankees took over first place and stayed there the rest of the way.

"That squeeze play with DiMaggio on third really hurt," Lemon recalls. "I knew it was coming. DiMaggio gave it away. He broke too soon. I threw the ball right behind Phil's head and he still laid down a perfect bunt. I tried to pitch it where he couldn't bunt it, but he laid down a blueprint and the game was over. It felt just like when you throw a good pitch and somebody hits a home run to beat you. It was the same feeling. You did everything you could, but it wasn't enough."

"Joe and I had a sign," Rizzuto said years later in *Yankees Magazine*. "Anybody that was on third when I was up knew my sign on a squeeze. I would pick the pitch I wanted to bunt on, and on the pitch before, when the umpire called it a strike, I'd argue. I'd drop the bat and pick it up with one hand over the end of the bat and the other hand just like you'd (normally) hold the bat. Then I'd get in the box. All that was the sign. The guy on third had to answer me by just rubbing his hand down his pants. As the pitcher wound up, the guy came home, and I could bunt the ball even if they pitched out. On that pitch Lemon threw at my head, and if I didn't bunt it would have hit me in the head."

Bunting in key situations, of course, was nothing new for Rizzuto. His ability to lay down a perfect bunt for either a hit, a squeeze, or a sacrifice, was by now legendary throughout baseball. "I remember how great a bunter he was," says Pee Wee Reese. "He didn't bunt the orthodox way. He'd flip the bat out. It was kind of like a chop. He didn't turn around or anything like that to let the pitcher know what he was doing. He'd just flop the bat down. I ended up doing the same thing. I aped him a little bit there. I would watch him and I finally perfected— well, I was never as good as he was — the bunt. But I got a lot of base hits that way."

"He used the squeeze against us on several occasions," notes Lou Boudreau, the former Indians' manager. "He was successful many times because he could drop that bat on the ball quicker than anybody. He would not give it away. You didn't know it was coming. It was mostly a surprise, which is what a squeeze is all about. But it is so important to time it perfectly, otherwise a pitcher will try and knock the hitter down or not start his windup in the first place."

Others, however, felt that Phil's bunting exploits may have overshadowed his ability to bang the ball around. "He was a good bunter, yeah, but for a little man, he was a very good hitter," says Yogi Berra. "He could make contact. People also forget that he was good in rundowns, boy. It would take five minutes to get him out. He was quick with those short little steps of his."

"He was a good bunter, but really I never recalled him bunting all that much compared to the amount of talking about it," adds Bobby Brown, now the American League president. "He could push and drag a bunt for base hits but he was a pretty darn good hitter, too. He could hit the ball to right field and he could pull the ball and in his prime, could hit maybe 10 home runs a year. He is a complete ball player. All you have to do is look it up."

The Yankees had a different look in 1951, with Mickey Mantle and Gil McDougald joining the club. It would also become DiMaggio's final season (he hit .263), making Rizzuto the last Yankee from the early 1940s to stand the test of time. New York won a third straight pennant, finishing five games ahead of Cleveland. Among the season's highlights were two no-hitters by Allie Reynolds, over Cleveland on July 12, and Boston on September 28. Rizzuto was a starter on the All-Star team for the second consecutive year and went 0-for-1 before giving way to Chico Carrasquel of the White Sox. There were six homers in the game as the Nationals romped, 8-3, in the game played in Detroit.

In the World Series, it was the Yankees against their neighborhood rivals, the New York Giants, and former Dodger manager Leo Durocher. The Giants, of course, defeated Brooklyn for the pennant when Bobby Thomson hit a ninth-inning home run off Ralph Branca in what became known as "The Shot Heard 'Round the World." The Yankees won the series in six games, but it wasn't easy, even if Rizzuto had a terrific series for a change. Twice they had to come from behind for wins. The Giants won the opener at Yankee Stadium, 5-1, behind the seven-hit pitching of Dave Koslo. The Yankees won the second game, 3-1, as Eddie Lopat limited the Giants to five hits, and Joe Collins slugged a homer.

On to the Polo Grounds, and the Giants took Game 3, 6-2. There was an anxious moment in the fifth inning of the game. The Giants' Eddie Stanky led off the inning with a walk, and with Al Dark up, attempted to steal on a muffed hit-and-run play. Stanky, who appeared to be out by a country mile, kicked the ball out of Rizzuto's glove, and when the ball ended up in centerfield, wound up at third base. Stanky's effort sparked a five-run rally for the Giants. Over the years, that play at second base became the roughest—and most memorable—between Stanky and Rizzuto, who went way back, first battling each other in the Piedmont League. They remain bitter toward each other even today.

The Yankees evened the series at two apiece with a 6-2 win in Game 4 behind Allie Reynolds's eight-hit pitching. DiMaggio blasted a two-run homer to clinch the win. The Bombers dominated Game 6, 13-1, thanks in part to homers by McDougald and Rizzuto. It was the Scooter's second— and last —World Series homer. Hank Bauer cracked a three-run triple in the sixth inning to spark the Yankees to a 4-3 win in the final game of the series. The Giants, however, did have one last breath of air in the ninth inning. They scored two runs to move to within one of a tie, but pinch-hitter Sal Yvars's sinking line drive to right field was grabbed by Bauer for the final out as the "tying run" crossed the plate. Rizzuto had an outstanding series— his greatest ever—and was rewarded with the Babe Ruth Award as the Series MVP. Rizzuto hit .320, scored five runs, drove in three, and was nearly flawless in the field as he played the part of sparkplug for the Yankees. Afterwards, Giants coach Herman Franks had seen enough of Rizzuto. "They never would have done it without that little pest," he said of the Scooter.

The Yankees' success story continued in 1952, even without DiMaggio in the lineup, and with the loss of Bobby Brown, Jerry Coleman, and pitcher Tom Morgan to the military. DiMaggio wanted to retire while he still had something left, and all the players, including Rizzuto, admired "The Yankee Clipper" for his December announcement.

At spring training that year, rookie Andy Carey remembers his first impressions of Rizzuto, and a comical story that had Rizzuto shaking his head. "I was just a 20-year-old kid when I broke in," he says. "Phil was 34, 35, so he'd been around. I had a lot of respect for him. In spring training, George Selkirk, a coach then, told me I had a chance to go over to the major league camp and that I should make my presence known, to let those guys know who I was, that I was the third baseman. So I get on third and with my spikes I draw a line between third and shortstop. Phil was the shortstop and I said to him, 'This is my side, you stay on your side.' He just looked at me and smiled." Rizzuto took a liking to Carey and heaped praise on the youngster. "He was a great help to me. He made me feel comfortable and gave me praise after a good play," Carey recalls.

The Yankees won the pennant by two games over frustrated Cleveland, which finished second for the second consecutive year. Mantle, Berra, Woodling, and Bauer were the big sticks for the Bronx Bombers, with Allie Reynolds and Vic Raschi leading the mound corps. Rizzuto was again named a starter in the All-Star game, even though his stats left something to be desired. At the break, he was hitting just .258. All-Star manager Casey Stengel released his lineup to the press on July 7, and he had Rizzuto batting eighth. Rizzuto was joined in the starting lineup by fellow Yankees Yogi Berra and Hank Bauer. It was a rainy day in Philadelphia, and the game was called after five innings, the Nationals winning, 3-2. Rizzuto was hitless in two at-bats while his "alter-ego" in Brooklyn, Pee Wee Reese, made an out as a pinch-hitter.

Rizzuto, who was now making $45,000, saw his average dip to .254, and people were wondering if his career could finally be over. After the Yankees knocked off the Dodgers in seven games in the World Series for their fourth straight world title, rumors began to persist that Rizzuto was through. His 4-for-27 (.148) performance at the plate in the series didn't help. That World Series was highlighted by Billy Martin's incredible catch of a pop fly over the pitcher's mound with the bases loaded and the Yankees up by two runs in the seventh game.

Rizzuto recalled the catch in a *Sporting News* interview. "It was [first baseman] Joe Collins' ball, but at the last minute the sun got in his eyes, because that's the way the light is that time of year late in the game. Bob Kuzava on the mound was simply trying to get out of Collins' way. When I saw what happened to Joe, I felt sure that ball was going to drop, with three Dodgers racing towards home with two out. Martin (playing second base) came out of nowhere. I don't know how he could react so quickly. I guess I was numb with excitement at shortstop as he ran in. I didn't think he could get it. It was a tremendous catch."

Earlier in the series, it seemed as if it was destined to go Brooklyn's way. The Dodgers won the first game, 4-2, the third game, 5-3, and then took a 3-2 lead with a 6-5 win in Game 5. But the Yankees' pitching excelled in Games 6 and 7. Vic Raschi was a 3-2 winner in the sixth game, and 37-year-old Allie Reynolds was victorious in the seventh game (he also won Game 4 and lost Game 1). Mickey Mantle walloped a pair of homers in the series, and Johnny Mize knocked three to offset Duke Snider's four homers.

Following the 1952 series, a report came out that the 35-year-old Rizzuto would be retiring following the 1953 season, in part, because he was suffering from physical exhaustion. In the days after the 1952 series, Phil was admitted to Lennox Hill Hospital for observation, and it was then that the report surfaced. On top of everything else, the doctors diagnosed an ulcer. As to his retirement, though, Rizzuto countered the reports briskly in an Associated Press story. "That report that I'm retiring after next season, why, it's ridiculous. I figure I have three more years at least, left in me — that is, active play. Day in and day out. After that even, I don't plan on quitting baseball. I'd like to hang around, doing utility work, then maybe coaching or serving in some other capacity."

Stengel gave Rizzuto a vote of confidence in a short *Sporting News* story. "He's one of the few guys left who can beat you both ways — in the field and with the bat. He's one of the greatest shortstops I've ever seen. Honus Wagner was a better hitter, but I've seen the kid make plays Wagner never made."

The Yankees won their fifth straight pennant in 1953, again beating out Cleveland, this time by 8 1/2 games as New York won 99 in all. Five straight pennants for the Bronx Bombers, an incredible feat, even for the Yankees! Yogi Berra and Mickey Mantle had monster seasons at the plate, with Berra cracking 27 homers and Mantle 21. One of Mantle's homers cleared Griffith Stadium in Washington, D.C. Yankees publicity man Arthur "Red" Patterson taped the April 17 blast at 565 feet from homeplate.

Joe Collins, Billy Martin, Gil McDougald, Gene Woodling, and Hank Bauer all had productive seasons at the plate. In fact, every starter, except for Rizzuto, had at least 10 homers. For Rizzuto, it would be his last productive year. He batted .271 with 21 doubles, three triples, and two home runs. He played only 133 games at shortstop, his lowest total since 1948, yet his errors were up, from 16 the year before, to 24. He did make the All-Star team as a reserve and was a late-game replacement for starter Chico Carrasquel, who finished with a .279 average that year. Rizzuto was hitting .253 at the break. Pee Wee Reese was among the National League starters and rapped two hits to help the Nationals to a fourth straight All-Star game victory, 5-1.

On September 2, Rizzuto had one hit— a triple— scored a run, and helped the Yankees defeat the Browns in St. Louis, 9-1. After the game, he collapsed. Suffering from chills and fever, Rizzuto was taken back to the hotel and later to a hospital. It was ruled that he had collapsed from the swarming heat and food poisoning. As a precaution, Rizzuto was flown back to New York and missed a handful of games before joining the team a week later.

In the World Series, it was back to the Yankees and the Dodgers. Despite some outstanding pitching by Brooklyn's Carl Erskine, who struck out 14 in the third game, the Yankees won their fifth consecutive world championship in six games. The Yankees won the opening two games at Yankee Stadium, 9-5 and 4-2, but Brooklyn won the next two at Ebbetts Field. In Game 5, Mickey Mantle, Gene Woodling, Billy Martin, and Gil McDougald blasted homers, as the Yankees rolled to an 11-7 win that featured a belated comeback attempt by the Dodgers. Mantle's homer, with the bases loaded in the third inning, reached Ebbett Fields' upper deck in left. In the series clincher, Allie Reynolds came through on the mound, and Billy Martin laced a ninth-inning RBI single to score Hank Bauer for the 4-3 victory.

Rizzuto had a fine series, batting .316, and played admirably in the field. It was a sensational run by Rizzuto and the Yankees, the five championships having remained the standard of excellence.

"There is nothing like winning," Gene Woodling recalls 40 years later. "When you win, you have a lot of fun. We had a bunch of good guys. We got along really well and to this day are still pretty close."

"I don't think we sat around and thought about it," explains Bobby Brown. "I think it was expected that if you were with the Yankees you were supposed to win the pennant and the World Series. If you fell short, you didn't have a very good year."

"Whatever it was, we knew at the beginning of the year that we were going to be in the World Series," says Andy Carey, who played for the 1952 and 1953 championship teams and remained with New York until 1960. "A lot of the other teams expected us to be in there, too, and weren't surprised when we'd beat them in the late innings. We were just phenomenal in those days. We had a reservoir of talent. Our bench players would be first stringers on any other team in the league."

"There were things we never got credit for," adds Woodling. "We were an outstanding defensive ball club, for example. No one could come close to our defense and, you know, basically, a good defense will always beat a good offense. We didn't get any credit at all for our defense."

"You win five in a row you had to have a good team," declares Yogi Berra. "Don't forget we had good pitching, too. And we had good hittin'. They were always throwing their best pitchers at us."

"At the time I didn't visualize what we were doing," admits Woodling. "But when your career is over you start reminiscing and you say, 'Holy Mackerel!' You look at that lineup and it was a heck of a good ball club. And Phil, he was outstanding. He could bunt for the base hit, sacrifice. He could do a lot of things. And, of course, he was very quick. He was just a real good ball player. I think we would have been in trouble without him. You don't find many guys at short like Phil."

"Ozzie Smith is the greatest shortstop I've ever seen in my life, but Phil fits in with all the other great ones," says Gene Hermanski. "The guy had good range and he was with that club for many, many years. Wasn't he with the Yankees when they won all those pennants? Five championships in a row? There's your answer about Phil."

"A team does not win those kinds of championships and have that type of success without a topflight shortstop," points out Brown. "It's just a prerequisite (to winning). You can go down through history. Anytime you see a team with a successful run you usually find a shortstop that can play. Certainly the fact that Phil was the shortstop during all those years and that the

team was successful is not just some sort of accident or coincidence."

"He was very important to them even if you consider the
hitting of DiMaggio and the other power hitters," adds Boudreau.
"Phil held their defense together. Whenever there was a spectacular play needed, he would come up with it."

"He was always regarded as the sparkplug," says Jim
Ogle, formerly of the *Newark (N.J.) Star-Ledger*. "He was the guy
who made all of those big stars go."

Granted, without Rizzuto in there, the Yankees might
have had enough to win five world championships in a row.
However, you've got to believe that with him in there, winning
five straight was a hell of a lot easier. In the months following the
1953 campaign, though, Rizzuto began to realize that his Yankee
days might be numbered. Never did he believe, however, that in
just one short year, Stengel would aggressively consider other
options at shortstop. The greatest years of Phil Rizzuto's career
were now over, and the decline was underway.

"He's now been broadcasting, what, 36 years? We have what we call an IFB (internal feedback), where from the truck I can talk to him, or both the announcers at the same time, or separately. To this day he forgets that when I'm talking to him, he kind of thinks when he hears my voice it's like hearing Seaver's voice and everybody else can hear it, also.

"Almost once a game he does something in regard to this, and my classic story was a game (at Yankee Stadium). It was a real blowout. I don't remember who was blowing who out, but it was about a 10-run game and it was the bottom of the eighth inning and Seaver was talking. George Grande was not on the air at the time; it was Seaver and Rizzuto.

"Well, we try to accommodate Phil, if possible, by letting him go home a little earlier. So I said to Phil in his ear, 'At the end of this inning, you can let George come in and you can go home.' And his response, on air, was, 'Oh, I love you!' Seaver was in the middle of a sentence and he stopped cold what he was saying. After a long pause, Seaver turned to him and said, 'Well, Scooter, I'm fond of you, too.'"

—*John Moore, WPIX-TV executive producer, Yankee broadcasts*

8

A Career Winds Down

The 1954 season was barely over when Phil Rizzuto learned that the New York Yankees intended to cut his salary. Manager Casey Stengel had been souring on the staple at shortstop for a while anyway, feeling that the veteran's best days were behind him. Not one to wait until a player had totally lost his skills, Stengel had been considering a move for some time. He saw Rizzuto's performance in the 1953 World Series as Rizzuto's last stand, if you will. His performance in 1954 left a lot to be desired as his average sank to .195 with just 13 extra-base hits. Stengel saw this as the end for Rizzuto, or at least, close to it. He made this clear during the 1954 season when he tried a battery of shortstop candidates in place of the sputtering Rizzuto.

And so, in early November of 1954, Stengel announced that he would be making wholesale changes in the infield for the 1955 campaign. Stengel, still smarting from New York's second-place finish to Cleveland that summer, even though his club won 103 ball games, was particularly unhappy with Rizzuto down the stretch. He benched the Scooter late in the season and all but turned over the reins to Jerry Coleman. Willie Miranda, meanwhile, also saw plenty of time at short. Miranda, who came to the Yankees in 1953, played shortstop in 88 games, compiling a .250

batting average. Stengel did not see Miranda as the answer, either, and eventually considered shifting Mickey Mantle to short, a position he played in the minor leagues. The Yankees also had Woody Held down on the farm in Kansas City, and he was given a look late in the year. That winter, the Yankees sent Held to Puerto Rico for more training. There were a host of plans, but Rizzuto was not a part of any of them.

Rizzuto did not do much during the 1954 campaign, statistically speaking, to garner much support from Stengel. He finished the year under .200, the first time in his career he plummeted below the .200 mark. Three times before, he batted in the .250-plus range. In 1953, it appeared he was back on track, hitting .271 after a .254 season in 1952.

For Rizzuto, 1954 became a nightmare at the plate. Besides his paltry batting average, the 36-year-old suddenly lost what little power he had, rapping a mere 11 doubles and two homers. For the first time in his career he did not have a triple. He scored 47 runs and drove in 15, both career lows, by far. In all, he played in 127 games, but batted just 307 times. According to some reports at the time, his arm was not as strong as it once was. Third baseman Andy Carey concurs.

"There were times when Phil would go deep to his right and because of his arm, he would throw the ball to me and I'd throw the guy out. He would tell me to take anything to my left and I would take a lot of balls away from him, crossing over to make the play." Perhaps most embarrassing to Rizzuto was that he was often lifted for a pinch-hitter early in a game.

"I cannot do my best under such conditions," Rizzuto said in a *Sporting News* interview. "I am not like Moose Skowron, who can walk off the bench cold and wallop the ball. I have to warm into a game." Bill "Moose" Skowron, a 23-year-old rookie, batted .340 in 215 plate appearances.

In actuality, the Yankees, as a team, warmed quickly into many games. The 103 victories were the most won by a Casey Stengel-managed team, yet New York finished eight games behind the unbeatable Cleveland Indians, who won 111 games.

The race was pretty close until mid-August (Cleveland led by 2 1/2 games on Aug. 20), when the Yankees went into a mild tailspin, beginning with three straight losses to Boston. With the way the Indians were playing, a mild tailspin translated into trouble for the Yankees. On September 12, a Cleveland-New York doubleheader attracted more than 86,000 people to Municipal Stadium.

The Indians won both games, all but claiming their rights to the American League pennant. Cleveland was loaded with pitching that season and that was the difference. Early Wynn, Bob Lemon, Bob Feller, and Mike Garcia had wonderful seasons on the mound, while Bobby Avila, Al Rosen, and Larry Doby had superb campaigns at the plate. The Yankee pitching corps, meanwhile, was led by Bob Grim and Whitey Ford, while the league's best-hitting team got a second MVP season from Yogi Berra and other outstanding efforts from Mickey Mantle, Hank Bauer, Andy Carey, and Joe Collins. In reality, the Yankees played great. The Indians, who would lose four straight to the New York Giants in the World Series, played better.

Prior to the 1955 season, Rizzuto wasn't thinking about the Cleveland Indians. He was more concerned about his own career. Rizzuto's relationship with Stengel, already strained, did not get better during the off-season. Rizzuto, in a moment of jest (he said later), had told some writers that Stengel should have taken 12 1/2 percent of the 25 percent cut he was being asked to take, insinuating that Stengel didn't have a very good year in 1954, either. "Some writers thought I was serious," he said a year later in an interview with Michael Gaven of the *New York Journal-American*. "I have never had an open break with Stengel. No argument of any kind. There never was anything personal in Casey benching me. He simply thought he was playing the best shortstop."

In September of 1954, Rizzuto had bowed to the wishes of general manager George Weiss and began wearing eyeglasses on the field. At first Rizzuto refused to wear them, claiming his eyes were fine. To wear glasses was a sure sign that a ballplayer was on the decline, and other ballplayers avoided spectacles at that time, as well. But when Rizzuto heard that Weiss was behind the suggestion, he gave in. Glasses or no glasses, Rizzuto did not figure in Stengel's 1955 plans, at least as a full-time performer. Naturally, Rizzuto balked at Stengel's plans, insisting he could still play every day.

"I am still able to play full time," the 37-year-old Rizzuto insisted in *The Sporting News*. "But Stengel evidently doesn't think so."

Rizzuto reportedly earned $40,000 in 1954, and the Yankees indicated that they would seek to give him the maximum cut (imposed by league rules) of 25% for 1955. As far as the Yankees were concerned, there was not much in favor of Rizzuto. His arm, legs, and eyesight were not about to improve overnight. And because of Rizzuto's part-time status, they did not see the need to pay him a full salary.

Rizzuto eventually settled on an agreeable salary that winter, taking a pay cut in the process, but had full intentions of remaining the full-time Yankee shortstop in 1955. Yet, he had seen the writing on the wall. He made it clear at the time that he would be interested in managing someday, would even work as a coach for a couple of years as an apprentice. The Washington Senators, with Weiss's approval, even approached Rizzuto about that possibility before deciding on Charley Dressen as their manager. Rizzuto, realizing that managerial jobs were few and far between, began looking toward another post-baseball career—as a media person, either in television or radio—which more and more had appealed to him. However, as 1955 neared, it was his shortstop job that he wanted most.

But first to make matters worse for Rizzuto, on November 18, 1954, the Yankees sent six players—Harry Byrd, Jim McDonald, Hal Smith, Gus Triandos, Gene Woodling, and Willie Miranda—to the Baltimore Orioles in exchange for Don Larsen and Billy Hunter. The 26-year-old Hunter was Baltimore's main shortstop in 1953, when he batted .243. It was clear right then and there that

Stengel did not want to depend on Rizzuto, whom he observed as a fading star.

Hunter moved in as New York's No. 1 shortstop in 1955. It turned out that he was not the answer, either, hitting just .227 in 98 games. Stengel used Rizzuto at short in 79 games and Coleman in 29 others as he often pinch-hit for one or another in the late—and even early— innings of ball games. The Scooter managed to raise his average to .259. But he came up to the plate just 141 times (as a late-game replacement in many games, he was not afforded the opportunity to bat too many times), his lowest total in a season, and had only 37 hits, six of which were for extra bases.

The Yankees overcame their weakness at short with stellar performances by several other players. Catcher Yogi Berra, centerfielder Mickey Mantle, and second baseman Gil McDougald excelled with banner seasons, while pitchers Whitey Ford, Bob Turley, and Tommy Byrne combined for a record of 51-25. When the regular season was over, the Yankees finished three full games ahead of Cleveland to regain their familiar spot in the standings. It wasn't easy, though, as the Yankees were in a season-long tussle to the top with the Indians, the Chicago White Sox, and the Boston Red Sox. On Labor Day, Cleveland was in first place by a half game over the Yankees, with Chicago and Boston 1 1/2 and 3 games back, respectively.

New York moved into first place on September 16 with a victory over Boston, thanks to ninth-inning homers by Bauer and Berra. New York went on an eight-game winning streak that all but clinched the 21st pennant for the Yankees. Chicago came in third place behind Cleveland, five games back of first, and the Red Sox, doing a royal fadeout, finished 12 games out. New York hurlers led the league in ERA with a 3.23 mark, sparked by Whitey Ford's 2.63 (18-7). Thirty-five-year-old Tommy Byrne won 16 games, and off-season acquisition Bob Turley added 17. Berra had another MVP season, whacking 27 homers and driving in 108 runs, and Mantle hit .306 and drove in 99 runs. Bauer,

Skowron, and McDougald had excellent years, as well, and Elston Howard, the first black Yankee, hit 10 homers and batted .290 as a reserve. As a team, New York smashed 175 homers to lead the league.

Ironically, when it came to the World Series, Stengel turned to the experienced veteran, Phil Rizzuto, to play short-stop. The Scooter played in all seven games and responded with four hits in 15 at-bats (.267), stole two bases, scored a pair, and drove in one. In the field, he was perfect. Brooklyn finally beat the Yankees, however, taking the World Series in seven games. The Yankees gained Yankee Stadium victories in the first two games, 6-5 and 4-2. In the opener, Joe Collins clubbed a pair of homers and Elston Howard one to offset an eighth-inning steal of home by Jackie Robinson. In the second game, lefty Tommy Byrne scattered five hits to become the first southpaw to pitch a complete game against the Dodgers that season.

The series moved to Ebbetts Field for the next three games and the Brooklyn bats went wild. Roy Campanella cracked a homer in Game 3 as the Dodgers, behind Johnny Podres, hand-cuffed the Bronx Bombers, 8-3. In Game 4, an 8-5 Brooklyn win, Campanella, Gil Hodges, and Duke Snider smacked home runs. And in Game Five, Sandy Amoros and Snider homered twice in a 5-3 Dodger win. During the three-game stretch, Snider, Campanella, Hodges, and Carl Furillo went 20-for-51 as Brook-lyn scored 21 runs on 34 hits. Skowron homered, and Ford won his second game in Game 6, 5-1, before 64,022 fans at Yankee Stadium.

In the seventh, and deciding game, however, the Yan-kees' luck ran out. They fell, 2-0, as Podres outpitched Byrne, and Hodges drove in both runs. Specifically, the Yankees' luck ran out in the sixth inning. Following a walk to Billy Martin and a bunt single by McDougald, left-handed-hitting Yogi Berra swat-ted a fly ball deep to left field. It looked like the ball might have enough to clear the fence, but the left fielder, Sandy Amoros, although shaded toward center, chased the ball down and made a one-hand grab. He wheeled and fired to the infield, and shortstop Pee Wee Reese doubled up McDougald. Thus, the Dodgers had finally beaten the Yankees in the World Series, after five failed attempts.

"It was a little frustrating," admits Reese, of the Yankee dominance. "I don't think we went into any series thinking the Yankees were the better ball club. The Yankees didn't create any fear among us. Don't forget we had guys like Robinson, Campanella, Furillo, Snider, and Hodges. They weren't easily intimidated. But to tell you the truth, it always seemed like something happened. It started in 1941 when Mickey Owen, with one strike away for the final out, lost the ball. The Yankees came on like hell and ended up winning that fourth game. Had we won, it would have been 2-2 and things might have been different. Instead, the Yankees led 3-1. After two or three series, especially in my case, you start thinking, 'Hey, what's going on here?' In 1955 I'm thinking here we go again, in the seventh game. Podres is pitching a hell of a game and runners on first and second and Yogi hits the ball to left field. That's when Amoros came through to catch the ball and threw it to me and we doubled off McDougald. But when the ball took off, I said, 'Oh hell, this looks like it could be it.' I didn't think Amoros could get to the ball but because he was left-handed, he was able to get his glove against the foul pole."

The World Series over, the 38-year-old Rizzuto wanted to believe there was still life with the Yankees, but he knew within a few weeks of the end of the season that his future was limited, at best. He told Gaven, "My uncertainty has me bewildered. First, let's get this much straight. I would rather play ball than do anything else, and I think I am capable of playing for at least two more years [which is what he said two years earlier]. There's not a thing wrong with me and when I played last season I was much better than the year before. But then a ball player is the last person to admit he's through. So let's face the truth. I didn't play regularly this year, although I started every game of the World Series, and I think I had a pretty good series."

In the same article, Rizzuto considered his alternatives, should he decide to retire. "They tell me I have the voice for radio and television. I have had a few offers from that field. There have been managerial feelers from minor league clubs. You know, I managed in the Navy when I was a comparative kid a dozen years ago. I liked it. I would like to manage very much, although that job has its hazards. One bad year and they forget about you.

"Should I do like Joe DiMaggio and step out while they still remember me for a good World Series? Joe could have collected major league pay for a couple more years, but he made some good investments and called it quits while he was still on top. The United American Investment Co., a new insurance company organized in Atlanta, wants to make me a director with full-time duties. Gene Woodling and Joe Collins are already working for them as agents. The American Shops, with whom I have been associated in Newark for many years, want to build a new store for men and give me a 50 percent interest. Then there's the bowling alley I am opening (with Yogi Berra) next fall in Clifton, N.J. [the two Yankees co-owned the alleys for several years before selling]. That wouldn't interfere with baseball if I were assured of playing regularly."

Rizzuto finally decided that he would, indeed, play another season with the Yankees. It was plain from the start that he would see little time. Stengel told Gil McDougald during spring training that he would be moving from second base to short, and Billy Martin would become the regular second baseman. McDougald responded brilliantly to the move, batting .311 with 13 home runs and 56 RBIs. In the field, he did fine, learning the position well. It was a strange time for Rizzuto, who played in just 31 games (30 at short, one game as a pinch-runner). He came to the plate a mere 52 times, knocking 12 hits, none of which were for extra bases. He scored six runs and drove in six.

In mid-May Rizzuto had a chance to win back his shortstop position and, had his play at short been up to snuff, he might have remained there through the season. Looking to make changes, Stengel started Rizzuto at short on May 16. Batting ninth, behind starting pitcher Mickey McDermott (who batted .212 that year; the former Boston pitcher was picked up by New York in February in a trade that sent Lou Berberet, Bob Wiesler, Herb Plews, Dick Tettelbach and Whitey Herzog from the Yankees to the Senators for Bob Kline and McDermott), the Scooter rapped one hit and drove in one run. In the field, he was perfect, as New York knocked off Cleveland, 4-1.

The next day Rizzuto, now batting leadoff, smacked three hits in five at-bats to spark the Yankees to a 10-3 romp over Chicago. He scored a run and drove in two more. In the field, though, Rizzuto had possibly his worst day ever. Rizzuto threw the ball away three times, as the White Sox scored three unearned runs off Whitey Ford.

A day later, Rizzuto had a hit and an RBI, but made another error in the field. In the ninth inning, Stengel lifted him for a pinch-hitter in a game won by the Yankees in 10 innings, 8-7. On May 19, Rizzuto was still in the lineup. He cracked a single and scored a run. But in the field, he was charged with yet another error. Rizzuto simply could not put it together at shortstop, and Stengel had seen enough.

On May 20, Gil McDougald was back at short, where he remained the rest of the season. In that four-game span, Rizzuto had six hits in 16 at-bats, a .370 clip. He scored two runs and drove in four. His fielding, however, left a lot to be desired. Stengel, unhappy with the five errors, sent Rizzuto to the bench.

In the remaining spring and early summer, Rizzuto would spend a great deal of time hanging out in the bullpen area during games. In the previous year he killed time out in the bullpen mainly for fun, but now, it was a way to keep his distance from Stengel. To the fans, however, he was still Phil. "In his later years, Stengel would put him in for defense and when he'd come out of the bullpen he would get an ovation," recalls Jim Ogle, who is now in charge of the Yankee Alumni Association. Finally, at the end of July, Rizzuto told reporters, as the team headed out of Chicago for a western trip, that this would be his last year.

"I feel great," Rizzuto said at the time to Dan Daniel of *The Sporting News* and other reporters. "But I know I will not be packing for many more of these tours with the Yankees. Why should they think of keeping me in 1957? Gil McDougald, with a great many years before him in the majors, has become the most valuable shortstop in the business. Then there are Tony Kubek, Jerry Lumpe and Bobby Richardson in the minors. I am going to talk with George Weiss when we return home. I will lay my cards on the table and find out what's what. My next shift has to be a move for happiness. Don't misunderstand me. I am just about the happiest ball player with regard to home and family. But I don't get to see my wife and children enough." Rizzuto took the time to let out the word that he could be in the market for a managerial position, if one existed. The Scooter, a staple with the ball club since 1941, figured he could relax now and enjoy his final season with the team, even if he wasn't starting.

The Yankees, meanwhile, were coasting in the American League. Eventually, they would win the pennant by nine big games over Cleveland. This was the year when Mickey Mantle came into his own. The center fielder won the Triple Crown that season, hitting .353, with 52 homers and 130 RBIs. In addition, the league's MVP led the junior circuit in runs scored with 132 and in slugging percentage with .705. During the winter, he picked up the Hickock Award for his trophy case. Berra slammed 30 homers and drove in 105 runs, while Skowron and Bauer cracked 23 and 26 homers, respectively, as New York led the league in home runs with 190. McDougald, as the regular shortstop, hit .311 with 13 homers.

In the World Series, a seven-game victory over Brooklyn, history was recorded on October 8 when Don Larsen of New York pitched the first, and only, perfect game in series history. Larsen, who won just 11 games that season, was brilliant in Game 5, and had been knocked out in the second inning of Game 2, a 13-8 Dodger win. The Dodgers, in fact, won both the first and second games, before dropping the next three. But Clem Labine hurled a seven-hitter in Game 6, taking a 1-0 pitcher's duel from Bob Turley. In the seventh game, Berra smashed two homers, and Elston Howard and Bill Skowron hit one apiece in a 9-0 romp that brought the Yankees their 17th world championship.

Unfortunately, Rizzuto did not get to enjoy the late-season heroics of his team, nor did he get to enjoy his season in the sun for very long. Dan Daniel recalled the fateful afternoon of August 25 for *The Sporting News* days later. "It was Saturday, August 25, at 4:30 o'clock. It was Old Timers' Day in Yankee Stadium, an occasion of jollification, of appreciation of what the old players had done for baseball. The Old Timers' program had ended and now the Bombers were taking a 4 to 2 beating from the White Sox.

"All of a sudden, a startling announcement was made in the press box. Phil Rizzuto, who had been with the New York club since 1941, once Mr. Shortstop, who had done so much to win nine pennants in past years and had helped some this season as well, had been released unconditionally."

There were immediate shock waves over the announcement. The press, fans, and players were stunned over the decision. When word got out over how Rizzuto was told of the release, the reaction was harsher. The Yankee great had been sunning himself out in the bullpen before the start of the game that day. Rizzuto received word that Stengel and George Weiss wanted to speak with him. The three met in Weiss's office. Rizzuto was asked to look over the Yankee roster and determine who should be let go to make room for Enos "Country" Slaughter, whom the team had a chance to acquire on waivers from the Kansas City Athletics for the pennant drive. Rizzuto looked down the roster and mentioned a couple of names. Weiss and Stengel shook their heads. Finally, it dawned on Rizzuto who the odd man out was. He was shocked.

"They had been keeping him on because he had been such a potent force," says former Yankee announcer Mel Allen. "But it's not like it (the release) happened out of the blue. In fact, by then he spent a lot of time in the bullpen warming up pitchers. At the time Phil was the third shortstop. They needed a left-handed batter and they had a chance to get Slaughter. They had to make room for him. They actually called Phil in to talk to him about what he thought about Slaughter. He was unaware at the time that the guy they were going to release to make room for Slaughter was him."

On his way toward the Yankee clubhouse, the dejected Rizzuto ran into Coleman. "I am released," he reportedly said. Coleman thought Rizzuto was joking. But Rizzuto convinced him that he was telling the truth. Coleman, like the rest of the Yankees, did not want to believe it.

Three ball players who were All-Stars that season recalled the day Rizzuto was released.

"When I played with him he wasn't in his prime," said pitcher Johnny Kucks, who joined the Yankees in 1955 as a rookie and was 18-9 in 1956. "He had all his outstanding years before I got on that club. [In 1956] we had McDougald at shortstop and Kubek was coming up. But it was a very sad day [when he was released]. When you spoke about the Yankees, Rizzuto was a great big piece of the foundation that made that organization so successful over a number of years. I felt sorry for him. When I came up as a rookie he made me feel real comfortable."

"He was such a great ball player," says left-handed hurler Whitey Ford, who won 19 of 25 games with an ERA of 2.47. "I'm sorry they ended his career that way. I felt sorry for him."

"We were all surprised the way they told him and everything," adds Yogi Berra, who was the American League's starting catcher in the All-Star game that summer and batted .298.

"It was cut and dried," remembers Andy Carey. "That's the way the Yankees did things."

But it was not, as Mel Allen suggested, totally surprising. If anything, Yankee management had a habit of making decisions such as these. When a move had to be made, it was made, no matter who was on the wrong end of the deal. A year earlier, Weiss got rid of Eddie Lopat, the former ace who slumped to 4-

8 at mid-season. Lopat, who went to the Orioles, had a record of 113-59, and four more World Series wins. But it didn't matter. As far as management was concerned, he was taking up valuable space on the roster, and Weiss acted. With McDougald, Coleman, and Martin available to play shortstop, Rizzuto was clearly expendable.

In Slaughter, whom the Yankees got from Kansas City off the waiver list, New York got a 40-year-old left-handed hitter with a proven track record of clutch hitting. Before getting Slaughter, pitchers Mickey McDermott and Tommy Byrne were often used for pinch-hitting duties. George Wilson had been purchased from the New York Giants, but he did not impress Stengel. The only other candidate was rookie Norm Siebern, but the Yankee manager was not about to count on a kid for the stretch drive. Ironically, Slaughter had played with the Yankees previously. He was obtained during the spring of 1954 and then was traded in May of 1955 in a deal that included pitcher Johnny Sain, for another hurler, John "Sonny" Dixon, and cash. Slaughter was batting .282 at the time of the 1956 acquisition. The bottom line was simple. If it wasn't Slaughter, then it would have been someone else. The World Series was just ahead, and the Yankees needed to make a move by September 1, when major league rosters were frozen.

The Yankee management certainly saw this move as vital to its pennant chances. It had nothing to do with money, since Rizzuto was due his entire regular-season salary anyway. He was also guaranteed a World Series share by Weiss, should the players not vote him a share.

To the Yankee brass, the move made sense. To Rizzuto, his loyal fans, and the press, it stank. Had he been released on a different day, perhaps, it would have been easier to take. But on Old Timers' Day, with its festive atmosphere, it did not seem fair. Some criticized management for not keeping Rizzuto as a coach, at the very least. However, league rules prohibited such a move, and the point was moot.

"I'll never forget that miserable day," recalled Rizzuto during an interview with Jim Ogle. "I was walking out of the Stadium crying when I met [former Yankee] George Stirnweiss. After I told him what was wrong, he told me he had felt the same way when it happened to him. He advised me to go away for a week, not to say anything I would regret and that it may turn out for the better. He left his car at the Stadium and drove me home. He was afraid I might jump off the [George Washington] bridge. I had been thinking about it."

Rizzuto didn't go away for a week, but he did disappear for 30 or so hours. When he emerged from hiding, he talked openly with the press. "I'd like to go into something connected with baseball," he said in *The Sporting News.* "But I would like to settle down and stay out of Pullmans. I have some TV and radio offers. I'll be doing something."

And, indeed, Rizzuto did get a number of offers. Frank Lane of the Cardinals made an offer to the Scooter for a playing contract for the rest of 1956, and a coaching contract of $15,000 for 1957. The Orioles wanted Rizzuto to join their broadcast team and had a deal on the table calling for $30,000 a year plus expenses. Phil Pepe of the *New York Daily News* reported in 1974 that Rizzuto was approached about joining the Dodger organization as a player.

Rizzuto balked at that deal when he was told he'd first have to go to Montreal until a roster spot could be found. While he considered his options during the tail end of the season, he wasn't about to make any hard decisions just yet. It would have been an interesting twist had he somehow ended up with Brooklyn, joining Pee Wee Reese, and playing against his old teammates in the World Series.

As it turned out, Slaughter had a great series for New York, rapping seven hits in 20 at-bats. The outfielder walloped a homer, scored six runs, and drove in four, helping the Yankees take the classic in seven games. The World Series memories that year were overshadowed, though, by one spectacular event—Larsen's perfect game.

Years later it was easy for people to recall the Rizzuto of old, the little shortstop who could turn the double play as quickly as anybody, the guy who had a knack for nipping a runner at first, the player who could kill you with a bunt.

"The main thing is that I felt he played shortstop as well as it could be played," says Bobby Brown, who played with Rizzuto for eight seasons. "I've never seen anybody who could play shortstop as well as he could play it. As far as playing shortstop, he was as good as anybody."

"I saw him play when I was a kid," says National League president Bill White, who worked as an announcer with Rizzuto for 18 years. "I'm from Cleveland. We hated the Yankees because they always beat the Indians, although Cleveland won the pennant in '48 and again in '54. They [the Indians] had some pretty good players back then. They had Garcia, Wynn, Rosen, Avila, Boudreau, Hegan. They had three, four 20-game winners. They played decent baseball but the Yankees played better.

"I didn't like Rizzuto. He played on a team that beat the Indians. Son of a gun, he played good defense. He bunted, he was quick. He was a lot better fielder than Boudreau, although Boudreau was a better hitter. I don't think very many people had the range that Rizzuto had."

"To me, he was a hell of a shortstop," adds Allie Clark, who played with and against the Yankees. "As far as I'm concerned, he was a great little shortstop. He could throw and he was a pretty good hitter, too." Clark played with Boudreau during several of the Indian shortstop's biggest years. "Lou was a better hitter, more power than anything. Lou knew how to play the hitters better, but Phil covered a lot of ground. Boudreau had the better arm, but Phil could get the ball released faster. They were both great ball players."

"I wouldn't say it was the strongest arm," agrees Tommy Henrich. "That's true. He didn't have the strongest arm, but he'd go in the hole between shortstop and third base. I don't know who in the heck had the strongest arm. I just don't know. Marty Marion had a pretty darn good arm. I always admired Pee Wee

Reese with his arm. He was a beautiful thrower. But Phil, man, he was poetry in motion. He just glided around. He was nimble. No doubt about that. He could twist his body around and get in position to make some great plays. I'll tell you, boy, he was very well respected. He took Frank Crosetti's place, and rightfully so. He earned it and went on from there."

"I remember him being an outstanding shortstop in terms of being able to make the double play," notes pitcher Johnny Kucks. "And he was a heck of a bunter, too."

"Phil was very good to the rookies," says Clark. "Phil was a great bunter. He'd get all the young guys together and teach them the art. He didn't have to do it. He tried to help them out. He was always nice to them."

"He was a heck of a ball player," points out Yogi Berra. "Heck, he was good. He was a good defensive player. Good fielder, very good. He could get rid of the ball really quick. You knew he didn't have a strong arm, but he had just enough to get you. He was a good bunter, too. For a little man, he was a very good hitter. He'd make contact and he was quick. If he played today, he could have stolen a lot more bases."

As it was, Rizzuto finished his career with 149 stolen bases, which ranks him 11th on the all-time Yankee list. In fact, Rizzuto is still ranked among the all-time Yankee leaders in many categories. He is 10th in games played, 11th in at-bats, 14th in runs scored, 12th in hits, 17th in doubles, and 16th in triples. His 1950 batting average of .324 remains the highest for a Yankee shortstop in a single season. In addition to his MVP season in 1950, Rizzuto was selected to five All-Star teams, made *The Sporting News* All-Star team four times, and was given the Babe Ruth Award for his World Series performance of 1951.

When the end came, Rizzuto's play resembled little of his heyday seasons. His bat was all but gone, his fielding was suspect, and his legs had lost a couple of steps. But he was still Phil. One of the greatest of Yankees to wear pinstripes.

As far as the New York Yankees are concerned, even today, he is considered the best shortstop to play in the Bronx.

"One time in Seattle at this beautiful round hotel . . . round rooms and everything. (Fran) Healy got on one of those kicks. 'What did you do last night, Phil?' I said: 'Well, I didn't like the room I had.' He said, 'Why?' I said, 'Well, it was a round room and I couldn't corner my wife.' Well! You should have seen the mail I got and the calls! They all liked it, but the station didn't too much."

And Cora? "Whoa! She didn't like it. She does not want me to mention her name. Once, a game was going into extra innings and I knew she was shopping and I said on the air, 'You know, if any of you people are walking with a radio along Fifth Avenue and see my bride, tell her I'm going to be late for dinner.' Sure enough, somebody said something to her and ohhhh! She told me later, 'Leave my name out of it.'"

—*Phil Rizzuto, Inside Sports*

9

To the Booth

If there was one favor Yankee manager Casey Stengel did for Phil Rizzuto during his final seasons, it was to let him get a taste of the broadcast booth. During games in which Rizzuto had been removed, Stengel allowed the popular Yankee to join Mel Allen and Red Barber in the booth.

"Announcing began to get my attention about five years ago, as a means of staying close to the players and to the game," Rizzuto told J. G. Taylor Spink of *The Sporting News* in the summer of 1957. "In the last two or three years, Casey Stengel would rest me from time to time, and now and then Mel Allen would ask me up to the radio booth to give the play-by-play for a half-inning. That got me excited and I never missed when Mel asked me upstairs. I began dreaming that maybe somebody who thought I might have a chance to be a broadcaster would hear me (and offer me a job)."

In addition to his brief Yankee broadcasts, Rizzuto honed his skills by announcing Dodger and Giant games at home, with his television turned on and the sound turned off. "Even when I was a regular with the Yankees, I would go to Ebbets Field if they had a day game and we were playing at night, or vice versa. And I caught every game I could on television," Rizzuto continued.

In September of 1956, less than a month after being released by the Yankees, Rizzuto filled in for the ailing Frankie

Frisch on the Giants' postgame show from the Polo Grounds. Frisch had suffered a heart attack, leaving that job open. In Baltimore, where he had auditioned for an announcing job during the 1956 season, another position was available. Rizzuto, if he had his say, would have become a major league manager. He realized, however, how difficult that notion was.

"I made up my mind that I had to stick close to the game. I thought of managing sometime, but when I considered how few managing positions opened up from year to year, I could see that wasn't the kind of job a fellow just walked up and applied for," he told Spink.

Both the Giants and Orioles were serious about Rizzuto's talents in the broadcast booth, and made overtures to Scooter during the off-season. The New York club was looking for a third man to join Russ Hodges and Bob Delaney, and the Orioles' organization had switched sponsors and were looking to bring in fresh faces.

"I got real excited about that (the Giant job)," continued Rizzuto, "because it was the job I wanted right at home, but the Baltimore people had been so generous that I didn't know what to do. They (Baltimore) asked me down there to talk it over, and I was amazed at the salary. I think a deal was about fixed up, but I held off because they wanted me all year 'round, and we would have had to move there. The hitch was that our children were established in school up here, and then my family and my in-laws were up here, too."

While Rizzuto considered the Oriole job, the Giants filled their position. If Baltimore was too far away from home, then it's a good thing Rizzuto didn't take the Giants job. Following the 1957 season, the Giants—along with the Dodgers—moved to the west coast, the Giants taking up residence in San Francisco.

One day, Rizzuto was in a crowd with several Yankee broadcast officials. He recalled to Spink, "I was more or less kidding when I said they should hire me, because I knew the Yankee players and the American League so well. I didn't give that another thought until I got a call to talk business with them. They were thinking then of running a four-man staff, with me as a relief man mainly at home. No traveling? Terrific. I never was keen about the road. I like it at home. Finally, they hired me as a third man, full time, and after that I am a firm believer in luck."

"I was told (about Rizzuto) in the winter," remembers Mel Allen, who harkened to the day Rizzuto was released as a player. "They promised him a job in the organization, if he wanted it. They didn't say what. I don't know whether or not they knew what it would be. In the off-season, the guy who had been working with me, Jim Woods, was told they were letting him go to make room for Rizzuto."

On December 18, 1956, John Farrell of Ballantine Brewers, the Yankee sponsor for broadcasts, hired Rizzuto, joining the veterans Red Barber and Mel Allen. Allen had been associated with the Yankees since 1939 and was considered the "Voice of the Yankees." The native of Alabama was immensely popular and had a huge fan following, unheard of for a broadcaster. He endeared himself to the fans with his greeting of, "Hello there everybody," and his staple remark after a fine play, "How 'bout that, sports fans?" Allen was on hand in the 1940s with the first Yankee TV broadcasts, the first night game at Yankee Stadium, and for every other major step taken by New York during his stint, which lasted until 1964.

Barber joined the Yankees in 1954 after a dispute with the Dodgers, where he was known as the "Voice of the Dodgers." He left after a bitter argument with Brooklyn owner Walter O'Malley. Barber, who always was "sitting in the catbird seat," remained with the Yankees until 1966, when he was let go after bringing attention to a poorly attended Yankee game late in the season.

Although Rizzuto had gotten a good taste of the booth already, Ballantine Beer representatives were not about to have the "rookie" announcer go in cold. Allen was told to sharpen Rizzuto's skills.

"They said to me later on that I should meet with Phil before the season started," recalled Allen. "We obviously talked about the mechanics of the (broadcast) game. It took him a while to get the mechanics. In other words, giving the count on the batter, the score, the rhythm of it, that sort of thing. It's the same way as if you're first playing baseball. You don't jump right in and bat .300. You have to keep learning. He already had established his personality as a ball player. He was well known. It wasn't like John Jones coming to town. Now he had to get settled in (to the booth). But he had to learn the mechanics of the thing. It's a lot more than calling balls and strikes or telling the listener that it's a fly ball or a line drive."

Rizzuto, like many other novices, did have his troubles during the early part of the 1957 campaign. "Oh, he made a lot of mistakes in the beginning," remembers Andy Carey, the Yankee third baseman in 1957. "But 36 years later, he is still there. Phil has done a good job, but not initially. He had to work at it." Rizzuto himself admitted to Spink that he was "very uncomfortable" for about three weeks. "It took me that long to get the hang of a clear, smooth account, because I had been hurrying and using too many words. I guess I tried too hard and pressed too much when I would listen to Mel Allen and Red Barber and hear them roll it out so easy.

"When I started I found myself umpiring and scoring, as well as trying to tell what had happened. It was something like talking to myself. On a pitch, I would yell, 'That's a strike,' and then the umpire would call it a ball. On a grounder which might be a hit or an error, I made the mistake of giving my opinion spontaneously instead of waiting on the game scorer's judgment.

"Naturally that couldn't go on for long, and I was out of the habit fast. What I was doing was anticipating the play, which I learned later was a common mistake for a rookie in my business. Have you ever tried to tell people exactly what happens the minute it happens? I thought it was easy. It isn't, or at least it wasn't for me."

The transition from ball player to announcer was a smooth one in terms of dealing with his former teammates. Johnny Kucks recalls that "Phil was good to get along with as an announcer. We related to all the announcers very well. We did interviews with them. Phil was a very easy guy to work with. He still is."

As the 1957 season progressed, Rizzuto improved and got another major break when the CBS radio network offered him the opportunity to do a nightly show. Rizzuto accepted the offer, and "It's Sports Time with Phil Rizzuto" commenced on over 200 stations nationwide. The show, sponsored by Winston cigarettes three nights a week and Val Cream three other nights, ran for five minutes, from 7:00 to 7:05.

Rizzuto offered sports news, sports celebrities, and his own opinions. In one 1963 show, for example, Rizzuto's topic was beanballs. During his career, he was beaned three times. Spurred by recent incidents in baseball that summer, Rizzuto said, "If I was commissioner of baseball, I'd automatically bar for life any pitcher who throws deliberately at a man's head and I'd fire the order-giving manager with him." Rizzuto recalled one harrowing experience he had. "I'd been a major leaguer more than 10 years the first time I realized that I was going to be knocked down. It was in 1953 or 1954. There was a time back then when I hit pretty good. And this day I heard a major league manager order his pitcher to stick it in my ear. I honestly thought he was fooling. I tried to grin and stepped out of the box and glanced at the catcher, one of the finest men I knew. But the catcher wasn't grinning. 'Phil,' he said, 'stay loose. I've got my orders. You're to go down.'

"As a guy who, in previous years, spent two separate tricks in the hospital with concussions due to beanings, you can imagine my feelings on the worth of the head pitch. Well, I stayed loose and that day I didn't go down for good. But if the intent wasn't there, I'm Sonny Liston."

With the CBS deal in hand, Rizzuto was not only a personality in the New York area, but also throughout the country. Financially, he was on the moon. In one newspaper's "Did You Know" section, it reported that "Phil Rizzuto, in his first year as a broadcaster, will make more money than he ever did as a Yankee star . . ."

The CBS show ended in 1976, but not his days in the Yankee broadcast booth. Thirty-six years after he started, he is still broadcasting Yankee games. He has long since vacated the radio booth, but remains in the TV booth. It has been an amazing run, with Phil sharing the booth with many announcers. Besides Allen and Barber, Rizzuto shared air time with Jerry Coleman, Curt Gowdy, Joe Garagiola, Frank Messer, Bob Gamere, Whitey Ford, Fran Healy, Bill White, Spencer Ross, Jim Kaat, Billy Martin, George Grande, and to this day, with Bobby Murcer and Tom Seaver.

In the early part of his broadcast career, Rizzuto wasted little time in offering his own variety of announcing. Even back then, Phil would announce birthdays, anniversaries, or special occasions, and perhaps give a critique of a cannoli he ate that afternoon. To Mel Allen, it was sometimes hard to take.

"He had his own ideas of doing certain things," Allen says. "Like the birthday routine. That was not my way of doing things. I was used to network stuff on CBS. You just don't do that kind of thing (on network broadcasts). It was his own style. It took a while for people to get adjusted to that style, which is not the normal way of doing a game. We all like to have a little fun here and there depending on the game, but we never had a list of birthdays. The game was primary. Let's put it that way. To Phil, the game was secondary. That's not criticism on my part. I just mean that is his style."

While that style has won over millions of fans, it has also irked many others. That, and Rizzuto's "homer" routine. "Yeah, I'm a rooter," Rizzuto admitted in a 1978 *Toronto Star* interview. "But it's hard to be impartial when the Yankees have been my life. They really hate me up in Boston for that. One old guy there— must've been 80—took his cane to me once. Told me I made the Yankees sound like they could walk on water."

The Rizzuto style, and also his ball player background, did not allow him the full confidence of either Barber, or Allen. Marty Appel, a former Yankee public relations director who later became executive director of Yankee broadcasts and vice president of sports for WPIX-TV, claimed that in Rizzuto's early broadcast career "he was kind of intimidated by the presence of Mel Allen and Red Barber, arguably the two best there ever were. Neither of them really tried real hard to make Phil a broadcaster. They were from the old school of almost resenting ball players becoming announcers just because they were popular ball players. But Red particularly made it kind of uncomfortable for Phil in the booth. He really didn't help him at all."

In 1964, Rizzuto got a big break. He, not Mel Allen, was selected to work the Yankees-Cardinals World Series for the national broadcast with another former ball player, Joe Garagiola. Allen steamed over the choice and pleaded his case to commissioner Ford Frick. But Frick would not get involved, and Allen was left out in the cold. The previous year Allen had lost his voice during the last game of the series, and NBC did not want another incident such as that. "It was his first national exposure and he did so well with Garagiola, who lifted him to another level. It was only his eighth year as a broadcaster," says Appel.

"It was an incredible assignment to do the World Series in place of Mel Allen. When Garagiola moved over to the Yankees in 1965 (replacing Allen, who was fired after the World Series debacle), they were just naturally an entertaining team, an enjoyable team. Red (whose last year was 1966) didn't like Garagiola either, so now he was in the booth with Garagiola and Rizzuto."

Indeed, when it comes to broadcasting, Appel is a firm believer in Rizzuto. "He is one of the most lovable characters I've ever met in my life and one of the most underrated broadcast professionals that's probably ever been," says Appel, who joined the Yankees in 1968 and spent 24 years with the organization. "I don't exaggerate when I say that. Working that closely with him you appreciate the professionalism, the fact that he can go in there and record a promo or an interview in one take, no problems, just as smooth as if you were working with Ed McMahon, just to choose a name out of the air.

"He always likes to kid that he's still a ball player, that he's not really a professional announcer like those other guys. But all the years he's worked, if you think about it, people always say, gee, that White and Rizzuto, what a great team; that Healy and Rizzuto, what a great team; gee, that Murcer and Rizzuto, what a great team. And all of a sudden you see a recurring pattern there. Phil's modesty in the booth, unlike so many pros, doesn't let egos get in the way. He just brings out the best in virtually everyone he has worked with. It's a very rare gift and really it makes him an unsung broadcast talent."

"Look at the people he's worked with and he's made them better broadcasters," adds John Moore, currently the executive producer of Yankee broadcasts for WPIX-TV. "In an indirect way, he has shaped my philosophy on baseball telecasts. They've (baseball telecasts, in general) really become, too often, too technical, too overbearing with analysis. There's a good middle ground, not that every telecast should be Phil Rizzuto style. Somewhere along the line people have forgotten that this is still entertainment. It's still fun.

"We've (my staff and I) all talked about this, and the approach is someone goes to a game, what do they do? They're not analyzing every pitch. They're sitting there and they're talking to their friends and they'll say, 'Did you see that?' and 'Look at that!' It may have nothing to do with the game. Or, when things start to heat up, 'Should they walk this guy?' The point is, we try and do our telecast in that vein. I just know that when I go to a game it's not all 100 percent what pitch should they be throwing. My philosophy has evolved in 13 years of working with him, and 20 years before that listening to him. I know that when I'm downstairs (in the production truck) and suddenly I hear him say, 'Hey, Seaver!' it perks me up. You can tell right off the bat that it has nothing to do with the game. It's something he was thinking about earlier in the day, or somebody came up to him and asked him a question. It makes you perk up and listen. What's he going to say now?"

Bill White, the National League president, certainly fit the WPIX mold during his lengthy stint. It was perhaps the team of White and Rizzuto that was the greatest of all Rizzuto broadcast teams, eliciting dozens of hilarious and memorable stories.

"One day he got lost going from the radio booth to the television booth, which happen to be right next door to each other (at Yankee Stadium)," recalls White. "One time in Milwaukee he introduced himself as Phil White. That broke us up. Luckily we were on tape. They played the tape later on. And everybody knows the story how I had left the booth and came back and asked to see his scorecard and I looked at it and started copying it and all of a sudden I saw WW. I asked him what does that mean and he said, 'I don't know. I wasn't watching.'"

But it went beyond funny stories between the broadcast partners. White recalls his broadcast relationship with Rizzuto.

"First of all, as soon as I went down to spring training I talked to Ellie Howard about Phil," says White, who joined Rizzuto and Frank Messer in 1971. "Everything he said was positive. Ellie really liked Phil. Evidently, Phil treated him extremely well when he became a Yankee. (Howard joined the Yankees in 1955; he was the first black to play for the Yankees). Ellie gave me my scouting report.

"I had never broadcast before so I probably didn't know he was such a Yankee fan. I didn't understand that," concedes White, a National Leaguer who played mostly with the Cardinals and Phillies in the early 1960s. "I had enough trouble trying to learn how to broadcast. I was more worried about technique than what was actually happening. First year, for instance, I just concentrated on the situation and giving the score. So, on a scale of probably 0-10, I was probably a 2. Phil would help me with some of the techniques and timing, differences in the leagues, umpires—some of them were quick calling balls and strikes, some of them were slow.

"For all those 18 years, number one, we had a lot of fun. I learned a lot and at no point did we have a cross word for each other. It was 18 years of fun and friendship. I had an opportunity to meet his wife. Spent a lot of time with Cora and Little Scooter. We used to go to dinner two or three times a year. It was a great association. A lot of broadcasters are jealous of each other and don't even speak to each other except when they're in the booth. That never happened in the Yankee booth. There were no egos in the Yankee booth while we were there.

"We probably got along so well because we were never together on the road. He liked to play golf. I like to fish, play tennis. We didn't have an opportunity to argue about golf scores or chat with each other playing golf. We were very seldom together on the road. Now we talk once in a while, but this job (NL President) doesn't allow me to see much of anybody. I don't even see my own kids. It keeps you busy. We have lunch together a couple times a year and we talk on the phone four to five times a year. But that's it."

Johnny Kucks has remained loyal to the Yankees over the years, and from his North Jersey home he watches Yankee telecasts religiously.

"I enjoy Phil very much as an announcer," he says. "I probably enjoyed him more when he and Bill White were announcing, where they would banter back and forth. That was good to listen to."

"I liked it when Bill White was on with him," adds Yogi Berra, who also lives in New Jersey. "They really had a nice time."

Since 1991, Rizzuto has worked with Bobby Murcer and Tom Seaver, a trio that has blended well together. Continuing the Yankee tradition on WPIX, the three have teamed up for a laid-back broadcast approach that sometimes gives a helter-skelter impression.

"Working with Phil is a hoot," says Murcer. "You never know what's going to happen."

"It may seem like it's crazy (in the booth), but it's not," adds Seaver. "It's a lot of spontaneity, a lot of humor, and a real lot of the essence of what is Yankee history."

Rizzuto has called many great games over the years, but the three moments he has said are among the most vivid are

Roger Maris's 61st home run in 1961, Bucky Dent's playoff-winning homer against Boston for the 1978 flag, and Chris Chambliss's pennant-clinching, 9th-inning homer to beat Kansas City in the 1976 playoffs.

Who can ever forget his call of Maris's 61st homer, off Tracy Stallard of the Boston Red Sox. "Here comes Roger Maris. They're standing up, waiting to see if Roger is going to get his Number 61. Here's the windup . . . the pitch to Roger . . . way outside, ball one. The fans are starting to boo. Low, ball two. That one was in the dirt. And the boos get louder. Two balls, no strikes on Roger Maris. Here's the windup . . . fastball. Hit deep to right, this could do it! Way back there! Holy Cow, he did it! Sixty-one home runs!"

Almost every year, it seems, there are rumors that this will be Phil's last season in the booth. A few years ago, when the Madison Square Garden cable network bought the television rights to Yankee games, it seemed a distinct possibility. MSG was threatening to have all Yankee games shown on its network. That would have left Rizzuto without a job. But eventually, a TV deal with WPIX was worked out, and Phil remains an integral part of the broadcast scene.

There have been other times when the Scooter has indicated that he'd like to retire, but it never seems to happen. Perhaps the closest time, or so it seemed, was back in July 1982. It was reported in the *New York Post* that 1982 would be Phil's last. Maury Allen of the *Post* apparently approached Rizzuto, and inquired as to the former shortstop's long-term plans, and Phil responded that he would be stepping down at the end of the season. A day later, Rizzuto insisted he was only kidding, that he never thought Allen would believe him.

This last rift pales in comparison to some real-life misadventures for Phil in his post-playing career. There have been more than a few other, more serious, harrowing experiences for Rizzuto.

In the winter of 1963, the Scooter was trying to clear out his snowblower. Instead, his snowblower cleared him out, eating up his right hand. When the damage was assessed, he had suffered multiple fractures of four fingers, two of which were very badly mangled. His wife Cora drove him to St. Elizabeth's Hospital, where he underwent three-hour emergency surgery.

The doctors did a fabulous job, saving all four fingers. The only setback for Rizzuto was that he was forced to cut down on his golf game, which he played seven days a week. These days, he hits the links three times a week. To repay the doctors, Rizzuto appeared as the featured attraction at a popular fund-raising event at the hospital, "Spaghetti Night."

Another time, in 1973, Rizzuto, along with Yankee players Hal Lanier and Bobby Murcer, was forced to remain in his fifth-floor Hotel Radisson room in Minnesota when a fire broke out in the middle of the night. Rizzuto and the others rushed out into the smoky hall but were told by a fireman to get back in their rooms. Ironically, Rizzuto had been on the 14th floor but requested a move to the fifth floor when White kidded him that in a hotel, the 14th floor is really the 13th. The fifth would end up being the only floor affected by the fire.

Ron Blomberg, who played for the Yankees from 1969 to 1976, remembers two more Rizzuto stories. "We had a special day for (former Yankee catcher) Jake Gibbs one day and Phil Rizzuto was out on the field getting ready to do an interview with (New York pitcher) Mike Kekich. Well, Kekich put a praying mantis on the microphone. Phil Rizzuto was afraid of bugs, afraid of everything in the whole world.

"Halfway through the interview, Kekich tells Rizzuto there's a praying mantis on the microphone. Phil actually ran into centerfield with the microphone. Nobody knew what was going on. Another time, Phil Rizzuto was on an airplane and there was a little bit of chop from turbulence. He got scared. He ran up to the cockpit and told the pilot 'You better land, I'm afraid, I'm going to faint, I'm going to die.'"

These are just some of the many tales that make up the Rizzuto résumé. When you look at the whole picture, it comes down to this: Phil Rizzuto *is* the New York Yankees. He is the one and only Yankee directly linking the past to the present.

"He is a guy who is really close to the Yankees," says Tom Seaver. "He loves the Yankees. He's been with the organization all these years and he's one of the only, if not the only, individual that connects the present and past and brings forward the great Yankee tradition. He is an integral part of the entire Yankee history."

"He's a legend," offers Bobby Murcer. "When you think of the Yankees, you think of DiMaggio, Mantle, and Phil Rizzuto."

"I think he *is* the Yankees," adds former Yankee catcher Rick Cerone, who first met Rizzuto at a baseball banquet in Newark, New Jersey, when Cerone was 10 years old. "I think he's great for baseball."

"In broadcasting, he is synonymous with the Yankees," says Bill White. "He is the Yankees. When you hear Phil, you hear that New York accent, you hear him rooting for the Yankees. From the broadcasting point of view, Rizzuto and the Yankees go together. A lot of people listening to him today probably don't remember him as a player. You're talking to a different group of fans. I'm sure a great deal of them listening today don't know that Phil was a great baseball player."

"I don't ever remember when he wasn't (a crowd favorite)," notes Marty Appel. "And I remember—and I was a kid when he was a broadcaster already—turning down the TV and turning up the radio to listen to him. That's how much I enjoyed him."

Working with Phil Rizzuto has been a dream come true for John Moore. "The only way I can sum it up in terms of both professionally and personally, is that it's been one of the greatest experiences of my life, to actually work with him and to be able to call him a friend. He's one of the most unique persons I've ever met. A lot of people ask me what he's like off the air. What you see on the air is Phil Rizzuto. That's him. He's a genuinely likeable person. Everybody checks their egos at the door when you enter a room with Phil. He has the ability to bring out the best in everybody around and puts everyone at ease. He makes them comfortable. He's perfectly willing to be the foil for somebody so they can feel better about themselves. He's just a wonderful person. I often think, 'God, I'm the luckiest guy in the world having been able to work with him.' I've got the dream-come-true job. I grew up a Yankee fan and grew up listening to Rizzuto. Now to have worked with him for 13 summers is something special."

As for Rizzuto himself, he, too, is living out a dream. He told Arlene Schulman of the Spanish newspaper *El Diaro* that he remains so enthusiastic "because I love coming to Yankee Stadium, or any ballpark for that matter, but mostly Yankee Stadium. And knowing that I am going to be doing a ballgame and seeing the ballplayers. I have spent my whole life here. You are lucky if you're able to do something that you like to do and make your living at it. I did it as a ballplayer and now I am doing it as a broadcaster. How can you expect to have more than that — to have the best of both worlds. To play in all those World Series and then broadcasting."

Holy Cow, Phil, you huckleberry, you can't beat that.

"In 1991 we were in Boston and I decided to take all the announcers out to lunch before we went to Fenway Park for a game. I thought, hey, let's go to the Hard Rock Cafe because it would be a little funky, Phil will talk about it on the air, and we'll have some fun with it.

"So I set up this nice lunch at the Hard Rock Cafe and Murcer came and Seaver came and (assistant Yankee producer for WPIX-TV) John Moore and I were there. We're waiting for Phil and waiting for Phil and he never does show up. So I see him at the ballpark later and I said to Phil, 'We were waiting for you. What happened?'

"And Phil said, 'Oh gee, if Cora knew I went to one of those topless places she'd kill me.' Phil is not always right in step with what is happening. But he's always cute."

—*Marty Appel*

A True Friend

No matter where Phil Rizzuto goes, be it the supermarket, the candy store, the Grand Canyon, or Yankee Stadium, he is besieged by fans. Rather than shy away from the attention, Rizzuto digs right in, answers every question as if he must. He is like your Uncle Bill, the kids' favorite uncle, the one with all the stories, the one you go to with a problem. He is the guy who can turn your day around, from a depressing one to an enjoyable one. To so many people, the Scooter is like one of the family. He is inundated with fan mail, "tons of mail," as WPIX-TV Executive Yankee Producer John Moore points out, and answers every bit of it. As he walks through a shopping center, he stops and talks with you. He is not Phil Rizzuto of the Yankees. He is one of us. Like our Uncle Bill, Uncle Phil is there when we need him. And he makes time, whether he has it or not.

"I always said that there isn't a person in the world that wouldn't like him if they ever met him," says Moore, who indicates that Rizzuto's friendly demeanor sometimes causes problems. "A lot of times, especially when we did Ft. Lauderdale (exhibition) games, there was no way for him to get to the parking lot or anywhere without going through the crowds. He hated it, and the reason he hated it was not because he hated to deal with people, but because he can't say no. He just can't say no. So what happens, he gets out there in the stands like that and he's out there for hours talking to people. A lot of times outside Yankee Stadium, he doesn't have the heart to say to someone, 'Look, I've got to get in, I can't talk to you now.' A lot of times when I'm out there on my way to the truck or back and forth, I'll see him talking to people and I'll just say, 'Scooter, we've got a meeting in two minutes,' and I'll leave it up to him. He knows what I'm doing. He'll either say, 'OK, my boss is calling me, I got to go now,' or he'll keep talking if he wants to stay with them.

"It's an amazing phenomenon. I know my mother just adores him. She's never met him, but she always tells me to say hello to Phil. He seems to get that reaction a lot. People say, 'Oh, my mother—or my wife—just loves him. Women just seem to love him. A lot of hard-core baseball fans don't seem to like him, especially if they're not Yankee fans, because he goes off on all these tangents. But a lot of other people just find him adorable because of that."

Rizzuto has not been on the field for almost 36 years, yet he continues to be a crowd favorite. When he played, he was honored by the fans on a few occasions. Banners hanging in the stadium proclaiming their allegiance to Rizzuto are nothing new. Ever since he put on a Yankee uniform, the fan adulation was present. While other former athletes moved on to another life, often disregarding their fans, Rizzuto remains glued to the ballpark and to his fans. And certainly today there are many former players—and current players, for that matter—who are still involved with the game, but turn a deaf, perhaps downright nasty ear to the fans. Not Phil.

"He was always popular with the fans," says Whitey Ford, who broke in with the Yankees in 1950, Rizzuto's MVP season. "They were always hanging signs up for him. Phil this, Phil that."

"He has such a nice way about him," notes former Yankee public relations assistant Bill Guilfoile, now the associate director of the National Baseball Hall of Fame. "He has remained very visible. Many other players, once they retire, they disappear. He is very friendly and makes a nice appearance. Phil has made a lot of friends over the years. He has a certain personality that attracts people to him."

"I don't know what he means to the (Yankee) organization as such, but certainly as far as the broadcasting team, he has been an integral part of it, for what, three to four decades?" poses

American League President Bobby Brown. "To the people who follow the Yankee broadcasts, I guess he's sort of like an old friend."

"There are a lot of on-air personalities who try and avoid the public," adds Moore. "This guy, he answers every bit of mail he gets. As you can imagine, he gets tons of mail. I've stopped by his room at the hotel on the road and he's got tons of mail in his room. I'll say, 'What are you doing?' He's answering his mail. He really cherishes and appreciates and understands that the fans have given him this golden career. He really tries to give back. He's really a special guy."

While Rizzuto certainly has many friends in the truest sense, there are many more people out there who feel they are friends with Rizzuto, whether or not he knows their name. It is all part of the Rizzuto aura. There is nothing wrong with this; indeed, it allows many people to feel as if they are a part of the Yankee tradition. The Scooter is quite accommodating and enjoys these "relationships" as much as everyone else.

Indeed, Rizzuto has proven time and time again he is prepared to go that extra mile to help out a friend. On the air, he often gives greetings to those in ill health, whether or not he knows them personally.

"My mother was very sick in the hospital," former New York Giants catcher Sal Yvars related at a charity golf tournament sponsored by Rizzuto. "She was very sick. She was quite a baseball fan. My father died very young. It was an oldtimers' game, and you know how busy Phil must be at Yankee Stadium, seeing everybody and signing autographs. And I got on second base. Phil is playing shortstop and I had told my mother I was going to play in the oldtimers' game. I say hello to Phil and he comes over and asks how I am and all that stuff. I say to Phil, 'My mother is in a White Plains (New York) hospital and she's going to be listening to the (regular Yankee) game. Just between you and me she's quite ill. Maybe if you could just say hello to Mrs. Yvars, get well, like you usually do, boy, she would love that.'

"Now with all the distractions he must have had, sure enough, he remembered. Anybody who would do something like that, I always think a lot of. As far as character goes, there are so many like Phil, but he's right near the top. He's right up there with the 1,2,3,4's, right up there as far as being a gentleman and being a very charitable fellow."

Rizzuto has had his share of special friendships through-out the years. In 1940, Sid Bordman was the 16-year-old batboy for the Kansas City Blues, the American Association team that Rizzuto played for prior to his call-up to the Yankees in 1941.

"We became good friends," says Bordman, who later became a sportswriter for the *Kansas City Star*. "In fact, he was sort of a big brother to me. I used to go up and see him at the LaSalle Hotel, where all the single players lived. He was such a nice person. I remember in the playoffs it was chilly and he gave me a sweatshirt or two. He just treated me like a little brother. He'd take me to a place called the Blue Bird Cafeteria.

"They had a deal there for the Blues players. They could go up there and eat as much as they wanted for about 85 cents. He'd take me there and a lot of other places. We'd go bowling. After he went back to New York we wrote to each other and then in (the winter) 1941 I visited him for about a week or so. That was before he was married, and he lived in Glendale, Long Island. He paid my way and I went on a Greyhound bus."

The two kept in touch by mail for the next three years, then resumed their friendship full force when the Philadelphia Athletics moved to Kansas City.

"When Kansas City got the A's in 1955 and Rizzuto turned broadcaster (in 1957) we'd get together all the time," Bordman says. "He'd come out to the house and he always stopped at a toy store—my kids were young—and he'd spend a lot of money on them. He was very lavish in his gifts. He was just a nice person to me. We still sit around and talk when he comes to town. Sometimes when he'd come to town, when he had the CBS five-minute broadcast, I'd knock off a script for him. He used several of mine while he was in Kansas City."

As a kid growing up, Anthony Schillizzi was a huge fan of Rizzuto's. He faithfully listened to Yankee games and his idol, The Scooter.

"I first met Phil when I was 12 or 13," recalls Schillizzi. "When I was growing up I was a big fan of his and the most depressing part of the year was when the season ended and I couldn't hear Phil's voice."

Schillizzi's friendship with Rizzuto grew, and in 1985, while he was still in high school, he began assisting him. "I was very friendly with Phil and started to go with him to games. I got into a routine, and more and more, I was with him."

Schillizzi—whose home answering machine features Phil's voice—helps coordinate some of Phil's activities and schedule, which, as you can imagine, is chockful of appointments. He also helps out with fan mail.

"Really, this is all very strange. I was always such a big fan of his, and how ironic, I now work for him," says Schillizzi.

Andy Stankiewicz, a gutsy reserve infielder for the 1992 Yankees, enjoys Rizzuto's friendship as well. Stankiewicz, who looks remarkably similar to Rizzuto, both in size and appearance, is glad to have people compare him to the Scooter.

"It's a tremendous compliment," he says. "I realize what Phil means to the Yankee tradition. To be compared with him is something I should be proud of. I'm nowhere near the player Phil Rizzuto was, but just to be mentioned in the same line—shoot, that's a great honor. I really respect Phil and what he's done for the Yankees, and I think he enjoys me because I'm a smaller guy doing well. I feel we have a good relationship."

In his hometown of Hillside, New Jersey, where he has lived since 1946, Rizzuto is an integral part of the community. Unlike many selfish ball players of today, Scooter is as giving as they come, often lending support to town functions, including an annual scholarship program for needy students at Hillside High School.

"He does quite a few things around town, from the Little League program to the health fair," says Vice Principal Al Lordi, who oversees the school's athletic program. "The Hillside High School Scholarship Fund has several contributors, one being Phil Rizzuto. Each contributor has an award named for him. His is the Phil Rizzuto Scholarship."

"Phil raises the funds by signing autographs at the annual health fair," adds Angelo Bonanno, Hillside's health officer. "He autographs baseballs and the residents supply pledges to the high school booster club (which handles the scholarship program; Phil and his wife Cora are official members of the booster club, although none of their children attended school there). In addition to what he gets at the health fair, Phil usually gives a fat check himself. Phil has always been available for any community project we've needed him for, from recycling to senior citizen programs to the health fair. It's simply a matter of availability for him. If he's available, he's never turned me down. If he's in town, Phil is right there when we need him. And he's never canceled out on us, either."

Bonanno recalled a winter storm in 1988. Hillside was launching a recycling program, and Rizzuto agreed to help kick off the event. He wasn't sure if Phil would be able to make it to the town garage. "We thought we might have to send a patrol car for him. But Phil found his way to the DPW garage. He came through. He's Mr. Reliable as far as we're concerned. He's that type of guy and it all depends on his schedule. Not many people realize how generous he is with his community. It's a little known side of him. The first year we had the health fair he came and asked if anybody was from the Little League. He had a check in his vest pocket and wanted to give it to the Little League. Just like that."

And, of course, everybody has a story about Phil.

"I'll tell you an interesting story," offered Hillside mayor James Welch. "When I was a kid growing up in Newark on the west side, about 35 years ago, I was in the Little League. There was a promo they were filming for United Way, I believe. I was at bat and Rizzuto was the umpire. I remember him saying, 'Now don't swing too close to that ball kid cause I don't want you fouling it off and hitting me.'

"Certainly as a kid you remember something like that. As luck would have it, as I grew up and became a lawyer and got involved with politics and eventually became mayor of Hillside, I got to meet him on a different level. I can honestly say that on the municipal level, whenever someone has reached out to him he has responded."

"I remember one year my daughter was selling Girl Scout cookies," recalls Bonanno. "He met her at the door and later I asked her, 'Angela, how did you wind up that far from where we live?' Well, she wanted to meet a celebrity and Phil, of course, was very gracious and signed up and did what he had to do. That's the type of guy he is."

Fourteen-year-old Calvin Spiker, a collector of autographs, was hoping to have Rizzuto sign a couple of items for him. So he, a friend, and his father drove by Phil's home in Hillside hoping to catch the former Yankee.

"I first got Phil's autograph at Computerland on Route 22 (in Union) at a Grand Opening," said Spiker, now 18 and a senior at nearby Union High School. "I was hoping he'd sign an 8 x 10 and some other stuff when we drove by his house. When we got there, his wife was outside doing some gardening and we asked if he was home. She said, 'Yes, go to the door.' And we did. He answered the door and invited us in. He was watching the Yankee game on TV. He showed us his awards room and we talked about players. We watched an inning or two of the game with him and he signed everything we had and we said goodbye and left. I've met a lot of players over the years, but he is definitely one of the more friendly ones."

The best "local" story of all dates back to 1983. Rizzuto, egged on by fellow broadcaster Bill White, could not name Hillside's mayor at the time.

"I recall the incident very well," says Lou Santagata, Hillside's mayor that year. "It was the opening of the baseball season and I don't know which mayor it was—maybe (New York City mayor Ed) Koch—was throwing out the first ball and White asked Phil Rizzuto who was the mayor of his town. He didn't know. He said that they are always changing mayors (true; the policy of the township is to select a new mayor each year) and he didn't know who it was at that time. A few days later it was the school board elections, and he wanted to vote. One of the firemen, a volunteer, said to him that he couldn't vote because he didn't know who the mayor was. And they made a big joke of it, of course. It happens that a few weeks later the historical society here in Hillside is having a pancake breakfast at the community center, and they invited Rizzuto and his wife. My wife and I are always there anyway, and we had breakfast together. Everybody made a big joke about it. The thing is, Phil had known me for a long time. He honestly didn't know who the mayor was at the time. So he went back on the air and for the next couple of weeks my name kept getting mentioned all over the country (Yankee broadcasts are extensive). A cousin of mine out in Ohio heard my name and called me up. 'Is that you they are talking about?' 'Yeah, that's me.' It was very funny."

Indeed, Rizzuto is more than just your local celebrity. He truly is a part of the community. "You'll see him at the local supermarket, the local deli, eating at the Mark Twain Diner in

Union," says Bonanno. "You'll see him getting gas at the Getty Gas Station on North Broad Street. He is well known to the business community. Everyone knows Phil around here and he doesn't dodge anybody. He loves people. So when you see that great big smile on the Money Store commercial, that's Phil."

Charley Shakoor owns the Hillside IGA supermarket and has had "Phil Rizzuto Belongs in the Hall of Fame" bumper stickers and Frisbees made up. "He is friendly with everybody. They walk by him and don't realize who he is and then they do a double take. They come back and say, 'Holy Cow!' He's friendly with my produce manager. He comes in the morning and they have coffee together. They talk about their arthritis and go through all the witches brews."

But they don't talk about the Money Store any more. After nearly 20 years, Rizzuto was dropped by the company in favor of Hall of Famer (how ironic) Jim Palmer this past March. A press release explained the switch.

Money Store Announces Hall of Famer Jim Palmer as new corporate spokesperson

Union, NJ—Homeowners throughout the nation will be learning how to take advantage of the equity in their houses from a new teacher.

Former major League All-Star turned broadcaster Jim Palmer is the new corporate spokesperson for The Money Store. He replaces long-time corporate spokesperson Phil Rizzuto who has appeared in Money Store advertisements for 20 years.

In announcing the transition, Marc Turtletaub, president and chief executive officer of The Money Store, noted that "Phil Rizzuto has introduced The Money Store to two generations. As spokesperson he made homeowners aware of the equity available in their homes and showed how this equity could be put to productive uses. Phil has helped make The Money Store synonymous with home equity financing. He has clearly been instrumental in our growth and success and we thank him for his 20 years of service to The Money Store. He is an important link to the company's roots."

According to Turtletaub, "Jim Palmer reflects a smooth, seamless transition. Like Phil Rizzuto he has developed a natural rapport with a national audience. He has a proven track record as a corporate spokesperon and will continue to reflect the same stable, comfortable relationship The Money Store has enjoyed with the public for the past two decades. He will closely identify with our next generation of customers and bring a fresh look to our long-standing television advertising campaign. We think he is the right person to represent the Money Store as we enter our second quarter century of business."

The Money Store, Inc., a national financial services company headquartered in Union, NJ, and Sacramento, CA, is one of America's leading home equity lenders, the nation's leading Small Business Administration (SBA) lender for each of the past ten years and one of the country's largest originators of student loans.

Although shaken by the decision, even though he knew it was coming, Rizzuto did not allow it to affect his relationship with fans and friends alike. That's not the Phil Rizzuto way. The Scooter is a friend forever and there is one Rizzuto friendship in particular that moves into another realm. This is Rizzuto's 42-year friendship with Ed Lucas. The story begins as a sad tale.

On a late September day in 1948, nine-year-old Ed Lucas was playing with friends at a Cub Scout meeting. Ed Lucas and another boy accidentally slammed into each other, their heads banging together. Lucas's left eye suffered severe damage. The retina was detached and soon he lost the sight in his left eye. Three years later, just days after Bobby Thomson hit the "Shot Heard 'Round the World," Lucas was playing baseball in his hometown of Jersey City, New Jersey, and a screaming line drive struck the 12-year-old in the face. His right eye hemorrhaged. In the days that followed, his family and doctors held out hope that his eyesight would be restored, but hope soon faded into reality. Ed Lucas would soon be completely blind.

"On October 4, 1951, I was hit in the eye with a baseball and lost the sight in my right eye," Lucas recalls. "I had lost the sight in my left eye when I was nine to another freak accident. I had a little sight, but it was diminishing. Knowing the love of the game of baseball that I had, my mother thought, to maybe boost my morale, that she'd take me to a store in Newark called the American Shops, where many of the ball players worked (as salesmen, but more to lure customers to the store). Gene

Hermanski, Ralph Branca, Yogi Berra, Phil Rizzuto, they were all there. Well, my mother brought my friend Gene Mehl and I out to meet one of the ball players to boost my morale. Scooter was there and I started to ask him questions and everything. He took an interest in me as a kid who had lost his sight. I guess my mother had told him. That meant a great deal to me. Scooter said come around next season to a game and see me. The next season my mother and father brought me to the Yankee Stadium and I went downstairs and saw the Yankees and he just took a personal interest in me. From that time on we developed a friendship."

It was a bit hard for Lucas to root for the Yankees in his home, though, considering his mother, and especially his father, were big New York Giant fans.

"I rooted for the Giants in the National League because my mother and father were big Giant fans," Lucas says. "Of course, I'll never forget the Bobby Thomson home run. I remember coming home from school. I could still see out of one eye. I was chewing bubble gum. My father, I'll never forget how he was a Giant fan his whole life and they hadn't won since the '30s. I walked in. We had a small TV at the time—eight inch, seven inch, whatever it was. He said the Giants were losing and Newcombe was pitching and I was chewing the bubble gum. Actually, he was sitting there with his rosary beads. After Thomson hit the dramatic home run he jumped up, he went crazy. He yelled out the window. 'The Giants won!'

"I loved baseball, always wore a uniform (from the semi-pro Eagles) that my Uncle Eugene (Furrey) gave me. It was a woolen uniform. I wore it every day. It could be 99 degrees out but I'd wear that uniform. Once I had detached the retina, my mother, unbeknownst to me, wrote a letter to Leo Durocher (after Lucas had met with Rizzuto). He brought me over to the Polo Grounds—June 14, 1952. I had already met Scooter and he had introduced me to some of the Yankees. Now here's Leo Durocher. He sort of gave me a day over there.

"I went into the clubhouse. I remember this attendant walked me into Durocher's office. I sat down in a swivel chair. Durocher walks in and the attendant said, 'Mr. Durocher, this is Ed Lucas. Do you want me to bring him around and meet some of the Giants?' Durocher said, 'No sir!' My heart dropped. I didn't know what to think. Then he said, 'He's my guest. If they want to meet him, they come in here.' And he had them all march into his office. Between Scooter and meeting the Giants, I'd drive my father crazy rooting for the Yankees in the American League, the Giants in the National."

While his relationship with Durocher was more of a one-shot deal, his friendship with Rizzuto flourished.

"Scooter was always there," Lucas points out. "He was there when I graduated grammar school (St. Joseph's School for the Blind in Jersey City), he came to my high school (New York Institute for the Education of the Blind in the Bronx). I started a club at the New York Institute for the Education of the Blind. It was a residential school; we stayed Sunday through Friday. I was amazed to find out that blind people didn't go to (baseball) games. So I started the club. Scooter came up with his wife Cora and spent a day. They had an assembly and I interviewed him. Another time we had Jackie Robinson. I was just into it. I knew then I wanted to do something in baseball." And more and more Rizzuto was part of his life.

"Scooter did a radio show (on CBS) and he did a little piece about me," says Lucas, who often feeds Rizzuto tidbits and trivia as ammunition before he goes on the air. "That was 1958. We'd speak during the winter. He'd call me up and I'd call him up. He and Cora and his family were always there for me, always encouraging me. When I went to college, Seton Hall University, he was there to give me a boost. I went into the insurance business and I take care of all of his insurance needs. Any questions he has, he calls me up. I've helped him out over the years."

With Rizzuto's encouragement, Lucas also attained his goal of being involved with baseball. After graduating from Seton Hall with a communications degree, he moved on to insurance but kept his hand in baseball. These days, in between his insurance business and his job with the public relations office at Meadowview Hospital in Secaucus, New Jersey, Lucas writes for a variety of publications, including *Yankee Magazine*. He also broadcasts a weekly sports radio show, "As I See It," over WOBM in Toms River, New Jersey. Lucas is a frequent visitor in the Yankee Stadium press box.

"The odds of a blind person getting into baseball or being a writer or a broadcaster aren't very great," Lucas concedes. "Let's face it, there is a stereotype that if you are blind, you can't do something. When I was a kid my stereotype of a blind person was a guy standing on a street corner with a cup. Phil encouraged me along when there were doubts, and he spoke to people (in the sports business) on my behalf. He had faith in me all along that I could do it."

"Eddie Lucas is able to do so many things that a person with sight can't even do," Rizzuto said in *Hudson County Magazine*. "And he's always willing to help someone."

Rizzuto, indeed, has gone well beyond the loyal friend when it comes to Lucas, including going to court for his good friend.

"I grew up in Jersey City and moved to Weehawken in 1954," says Lucas. "I got married in 1965 and moved back to Jersey City in 1971. After we moved to Jersey City, my wife walked out on me, leaving me with two kids—boys—which I raised with the help of my mother and father and sister. If it wasn't for them I would never have been able to raise them. Eight years later she came back to claim custody. When I first went to court the judge said, 'Ah, well, they'd be better off if a woman, who could see, had them.' The judge figured, you're blind, so what. My buddies in the Lions Club rallied about me and helped me get another lawyer. We got it overturned in appellate court. Scooter had never been in a courtroom, but he came and testified for me as a character witness, and I won custody of my two boys. Again, he was there for me.

"I can't speak highly enough about this man. The things he does that people don't know about. He wouldn't want me to reveal them. He goes out of his way for people. He does so many things quietly. He comes to my house just to chit-chat. Cora is the same way, a very quiet person. She's a wonderful woman. They were at my wedding, at different affairs. When I went to get my Seeing Eye dog—I've had four Seeing Eye dogs — he's been up there every time to visit me. He's a busy man, a prominent man, but he goes around and talks to people like you and I are talking now."

Rizzuto played another key role in Lucas's life, as indirect matchmaker.

"To show you how involved Scooter is with my life, about seven or eight years ago, he called me up and said he knew a woman who worked at a florist shop and she was concerned about another woman who worked there who was having trouble seeing," Lucas remembers. "This one gal working there hap-

pened to be a nurse and she was a premature baby. If you don't
know about premature babies, when they're in incubators, sometimes it can cause eye problems. Well anyway, this young lady
had eye problems, but she could see enough. She went on to
Seton Hall University to nursing school. She got a degree. She
was the class valedictorian. She worked in the florist shop while
she was going to school. Her aunt was so devastated, telling Phil,
gee, it took 30 years, but her eyesight is going. Scooter said he had
a friend who is blind, maybe he can talk to her.

"Well, I helped her out, I talked to her, I encouraged her.
I got her some rehabilitation. We never met. We talked on the
phone for seven years. Her name is Allison Pfeifle and last year
she called up and asked me if I could get her some Yankee tickets
for a supplier. I bought the tickets, and I said to myself, instead
of mailing them I'll have one of my friends drive me down.

"I walked in and she had seen me on television and had
seen some of my articles, so she knew who I was. I told her about
the (golf) tournament that Scooter and I put together and she
wanted to get involved. After that I asked her out and July 25,
1992 we became engaged. We're getting married November,
1993. She has partial sight and we get around. People think,
wow, how are you going to make it? Well, you have to have
determination. I don't consider my blindness a handicap. Scooter,
again, played a big role in my life."

Two years ago, Lucas and Rizzuto teamed up to put on
the Phil Rizzuto Celebrity Golf Classic. The tournament benefits
St. Joseph's School for the Blind. The tournament has attracted a
number of former players and entertainment figures, making for
a successful event in its first two years.

"I ran an auction (in 1990) and we raised maybe seven or
eight thousand dollars," Lucas said of the tournament's begin-
nings. "Phil said, 'Why don't we run a golf tournament?' I said
only if we could use his name. But he's shy about it. On the air
he talks about the Eddie Lucas Tournament. I tell him people
aren't going to come for me. It's a way to give back to the school.
These nuns, they did so much for me. They changed my life—
and my mother and father's lives—around. Unfortunately, the
public has a bad image of blind people. Right away they think
they can't do this, they can't do that. Thank God my mother and
father had faith in me. And so did Scooter."

"I remember one time they put a praying mantis on a micro-phone. It went all the way up the microphone. Rizzuto went up to the microphone and began speaking. Then he saw the praying mantis. He scooted out of there. Maybe that's how he really got the nickname Scooter."

—*Gene Michael, Yankees general manager*

"My Life is Not Complete"

Late in the afternoon of August 7, 1992, Phil Rizzuto works his way, as usual, through the crowd outside Yankee Stadium, signing autographs, exchanging greetings, and shaking hands with friends, and those who want to be his friend, as he enters the ballpark.

WPIX-TV will broadcast tonight's game against the Boston Red Sox, the franchise that has always seemed to bring out the best in the Yankees. While Rizzuto mixes with the crowd outside, Tom Seaver, one of Rizzuto's partners in the TV booth, is receiving congratulations inside the press dining room. A few days earlier, Seaver had been inducted into the Hall of Fame.

Rizzuto has won the American League Most Valuable Player award. He is a member of the New York Sports Hall of Fame, has been honored by the American Sportscasters Hall of Fame, was the first recipient of the Hickock Award for his 1950 season, and his uniform, No. 10, has been retired by the Yankees. In May of this year, Rizzuto was among the first 10 inductees into the New Jersey Hall of Fame, joining Yogi Berra, Larry Doby, Bill Bradley, Harry Carson, Franco Harris, Tommy Heinsohn, and others. In fact, Rizzuto has been honored by hundreds of groups over the years.

However, he has not been honored by the National Baseball Hall of Fame in Cooperstown, New York. It bothers him much more than he would like you to think.

As the sun sets over Yankee Stadium in the Bronx, Rizzuto is torn. He is thrilled for Seaver, who clearly deserves to be in the Hall of Fame after amassing a lifetime record of 311-205 as a pitcher for the New York Mets, the Cincinnati Reds, the Chicago White Sox, and the Boston Red Sox.

Before the game begins, Rizzuto poses with Seaver and the third man in the booth, former Yankee outfielder Bobby Murcer. The three of them hold up a huge cake commemorating Seaver's election to the Hall of Fame. Rizzuto smiles as Seaver opens a gift, a magnificent drawing, and he smiles as he takes his seat next to Seaver just before the first pitch is thrown by Yankee pitcher Scott Sanderson. Beneath the smile, Rizzuto wonders why he has not been elected to the Hall of Fame.

Ironically, almost seven years earlier, Seaver unknowingly took much of the thunder away from Phil when the Yankees honored Rizzuto with a day. It was to be Scooter's day, and his alone, when principal owner George Steinbrenner got the idea to retire Phil's No. 10 and to give him a permanent plaque in Yankee Stadium's Monument Park in left-center field (once dubbed "Death Valley").

The day was scheduled, in part, because the year before, the Hall of Fame's Committee on Baseball Veterans, or as it is more simply known, the Veterans Committee, voted to induct Brooklyn Dodgers shortstop Pee Wee Reese into the hall, but not Phil. Steinbrenner, who has voiced his anger repeatedly over the snubbing of Phil, was incensed in 1984, vowing to never let the Yankees play in a Hall of Fame exhibition game again (he relented several years later).

Indeed, in the "Who is better, Duke Snider, Willie Mays, or Mickey Mantle?" mode, there was the Reese versus Rizzuto argument, too. If one got into the Hall of Fame, surely the other deserved to as well.

Phil's plaque, placed among other Yankee greats in Monument Park, reads: "From 1941-56, The 'Scooter' was the Yankees' catalyst, leading them to nine World Series, his outstanding talents and enthusiasm made him the best shortstop the Yankees ever had." He is one of the best shortstops ever, Yankees or otherwise.

Back on that gorgeous August 4, 1985, Sunday afternoon, when Tom Seaver hurled his way into immortality and guaranteed himself a spot in the Hall of Fame, the former Met made Phil's day a secondary issue for many of the people who came to the ballpark that day. Pitching for the Chicago White Sox, the right-hander struck out seven batters and gave up six hits to beat the Yankees, 4-1, and gain his 300th career victory as 54,032 fans, many of whom were wearing Mets caps, cheered wildly as pinch-hitter Don Baylor flied out to Rudy Law in left field to end the game.

Prior to the game, it was Rizzuto's show. The Scooter was given gift after gift, but the one that got the most reaction was a cow, befitting his oft used "Holy Cow." This cow—complete with a halo—offered some comic entertainment when it nudged up against Rizzuto, and the former shortstop responded quickly by falling to the ground as the crowd laughed.

Old teammates Mickey Mantle and Billy Martin were there, and in another ironic twist, it was Murcer, then a Yankee executive, who presented Rizzuto with retired uniform No. 10. With that he joined Babe Ruth (3), Lou Gehrig (4), Joe DiMaggio (5), Mantle (7), Yogi Berra and Bill Dickey (8), Roger Maris (9), Thurman Munson (15), Whitey Ford (16), Elston Howard (32), and Casey Stengel (37) as those who have had their Yankee numbers retired.

And so, on a day that should have been all his, there was Seaver on the east coast. The same day, across the country, California Angel Rod Carew was making headlines with his 3,000th hit, and even Dwight Gooden was making news, winning his 17th game of the year as the crosstown Mets were taking a big game from the Chicago Cubs in the midst of a pennant race.

And now, here was Seaver again, seven years later, enjoying the fruits of his Hall of Fame induction right there in the Yankee broadcast booth, home of Phil Rizzuto for the past three and a half decades.

After the third inning, with the Yankees leading Boston in this meaningless game, 2-0, Rizzuto headed for his "office" for his mid-game break. His office, a hallway near the entranceway to the press box, and just around the corner from the men's room, is where Rizzuto entertains Yankee fans who have waited patiently to visit with him. There is a tounge-in-cheek sign in the hallway that reads:

PHIL RIZZUTO'S OFFICE
Open 7-7:30 weekdays
1-1:30 weekends
Autographing by appointment only
VISA/MASTERCARD & CANNOLIS ACCEPTED

While Rizzuto is being interviewed by a small group of college students, the Yankees have increased their lead to 4-0 on a home run by Bernie Williams and an RBI single from Matt Nokes. As the Red Sox are going down 1-2-3 in the top of the sixth inning, Rizzuto munches on a sausage in the press box snack bar and ponders an offer to do a book. He makes it clear just how much the Hall of Fame snub eats at him.

Explaining why he won't do his own book, Phil said, "My life is not complete. Maybe if I made the Hall of Fame this year I would've done one." Saying that he is public domain, and that anybody can write a book about him, he is not interested in sitting down and discussing his life in depth. Had he made the Hall of Fame, he might have felt differently.

Soon after, Rizzuto is back in the booth. Seaver has gone home to Connecticut, and Rizzuto joins Murcer for the last three innings of a game the Yankees eventually hold on to win, 7-5.

On the day he was honored in 1985, Rizzuto said, "This means more to me than being inducted into the Hall of Fame." A few years later, he told Arlene Schulman of the Spanish newspaper *El Diaro*, "That (not being in the Hall of Fame) does not bother me at all. More people are bothered and affected by that than I am. I know that I am not going to get in so I am very fortunate (because, supposedly, it is not a concern of his)."

But National League president Bill White knows the truth. "Phil wants to be in the Hall of Fame," says Rizzuto's former broadcast partner. "I've seen his reactions prior to voting and after the voting. It's really a downer after voting is announced."

Currently there are 16 shortstops in the Hall of Fame.

Shortstops	G	AB	R	H	2B	3B	HR	RBI	Pct.
Aparicio, Luis	2599	10230	1335	2677	394	92	83	791	.262
Appling, Luke	2422	8856	1319	2749	440	102	45	1116	.310
Bancroft, Dave	1913	7182	1048	2004	320	77	32	591	.279
Banks, Ernie	2528	9421	1305	2583	407	90	512	1636	.274
Boudreau, Lou	1646	6029	861	1779	385	66	68	789	.295
Cronin, Joe	2124	7579	1233	2285	515	118	170	1424	.301
Jackson, Travis	1656	6086	833	1768	291	86	135	929	.291
Jennings, Hugh	1264	4840	989	1520	227	88	19	840	.314
Maranville, Rabbit	2670	10078	1255	2605	380	177	28	874	.258
Reese, Pee Wee	2166	8058	1338	2170	330	80	126	885	.269
Sewell, Joe	1903	7132	1141	2226	436	68	49	1053	.312
Tinker, Joe	1642	5936	716	1565	238	106	29	--	.264
Vaughan, Arky	1817	6622	1173	2103	356	128	96	926	.318
Wagner, Honus	2785	10427	1740	3430	651	252	101	1732	.329
Wallace, Bobby	2369	8629	1056	2308	394	149	36	1121	.267
Ward, Monte	1810	7579	1403	2151	232	95	26	605	.283

Luke Appling (1930-50), Lou Boudreau (1938-52), and Pee Wee Reese (1940-58) played the bulk of their careers the same time as Rizzuto, while most of the others played before Rizzuto. Statistically, Rabbit Maranville, Joe Tinker, and Bobby Wallace offer Rizzuto little competition. While you can argue about which shortstops are and are not deserving of the Hall of Fame, to Rizzuto fans and many former players, the only one who counts is Reese.

In 2,166 games, Reese batted .269, hit 126 home runs, drove in 885 runs, stole 232 bases, scored 1,338 runs, and had 2,170 hits. Reese, who never won an MVP award, finished in the top 10 in MVP voting eight times (although never higher than fifth) and had a lifetime fielding percentage of .962. Reese was cited by *The Sporting News* as the outstanding major league shortstop in 1953.

In 13 years, Rizzuto played in 1,661 games, batted .273, stole 149 bases, scored 877 runs, had 1,588 hits, 562 RBIs, and smacked 38 home runs. Without a doubt, Rizzuto was the game's best bunter. He won the MVP award in 1950, played on nine pennant-winning ball clubs, and seven world championship teams. His fielding percentage was .968, with *The Sporting News* naming him the outstanding major league shortstop four straight seasons, from 1949 to 1952.

"I think they were almost identical," says Hall of Fame Yankee pitcher Whitey Ford. "Pee Wee probably had a better arm than Phil. They hit about the same and they both ran well. Phil was a flashy type shortstop. He'd make plays in the hole and get rid of the ball real quick. Pee Wee played shortstop a little different. He was more of your fundamental shortstop. He had a good arm. Pee Wee probably reminded me more of a Tony Kubek whereas Phil was the real flashy type. He had to charge balls and get rid of the ball quick because he didn't have the arm."

"Pee Wee was a good hitter. But I can't for the life of me figure that Hall of Fame business," adds former Yankee Gene Woodling, who was in the Navy with Reese. "Pee Wee is in there now, but I'd have to say that if you flip a coin, you got Reese and Rizzuto. Both were good ball players and they were very comparable. That's the best way to describe it."

"If Pee Wee Reese can get in the Hall of Fame then Phil should be in, too," offers Andy Carey, who played alongside Rizzuto during the latter part of Phil's career. "They were very similar. I think Phil may have annoyed some sportswriters because he wasn't real friendly with them. He wasn't a clique-ish guy anyway. We'd go on a road trip and we'd wonder what he was going to bring home to Cora. He'd always come back on the very last road trip with more presents than anybody I'd ever seen in my life. So I didn't think Phil got as good of press as Reese did. I think that might have hurt Phil. Over the years he has certainly proven to be a credit to the game. You never hear of any scandals with Phil."

Former *Newark Star-Ledger* reporter Jim Ogle is as miffed as anyone else concerning Rizzuto's omission to the Hall, although he agrees with Carey that Phil's relationship with the press may be a factor. "That's why he's not in the Hall of Fame," he declares.

"Today he is a character. Then, he was a loner. He kept to himself. He would disappear. He really wasn't a good interview. He was never a guy who pushed himself (to relate well with the press). It wasn't that there was a problem. It's just that Phil was not close with the press. He's got a closer relationship with the press now than he ever did.

"I was really surprised when he and Reese didn't go in together. Now he's in the hands of the Veterans Committee. I don't know what the story is there. There's a lot of (strange) things about the Hall of Fame. Look how long it took them to put Lazzeri and Johnny Mize in. How can you keep Mize out all those years? Allie Reynolds never got in and he certainly should be in there. Phil was the MVP, won the Hickock Belt, did all the other things. Even today when Phil comes out on the field he gets a big ovation. If the fans voted he would be in the Hall of Fame easy."

"In my neighborhood in Newark (New Jersey) where I grew up we called Rizzuto, 'Little Old Reliable,'" says Angelo Bonanno, the health officer in Hillside and a longtime fan of Rizzuto. "The guy was a fantastic ball player. No balls got through shortstop. He may have been a peanut, but he got his hits. That's why I'm galled when these second-rate players get in. The way I see it, this has got to be something personal (keeping Phil out). There's got to be something rotten here. Phil Rizzuto was a damn good ball player and he belongs in the Hall of Fame."

Back to the subject of Reese and Rizzuto, former Yankee and now San Diego Padres broadcaster, Jerry Coleman, told *USA Today*, "I don't think you can separate them. Reese had more leadership qualities; he was the blood and guts of those Dodger teams. But Phil did whatever it took to win. He could hit, run and field and was one of the best bunters ever."

The following two pages show how the two compared at the plate and in the field.

Billy Hitchcock played with Rizzuto on the Kansas City Blues in 1939-40 and also remembers Reese, who was a standout in the American Association as well, where comparisons to Rizzuto were first made. "They were different types of players, but they were both fine shortstops. Outstanding shortstops, in fact. To me, neither could miss."

"I thought at the time Phil was as good a shortstop as anybody I've seen," adds New York Giants reserve catcher Sal Yvars. "He was above our shortstop, Alvin Dark, although he was exceptional. And Phil was right up there with Pee Wee Reese. I thought he was as good, or better than Reese."

In Bill James's *Historical Baseball Abstract*, James describes the controversy this way: "Reese and Rizzuto were linked so

Phil Rizzuto
Career Stats

Year	Games	BA	AB	H	2B	3B	HR	R	RBI	BB	SO	SB	PO	A	E	DP	FA
1941	133	.307	515	158	20	9	3	65	46	27	36	14	252	399	29	109	.957
1942	144	.284	553	157	24	7	4	79	68	44	40	22	324	445	30	114	.962
1946	126	.257	471	121	17	1	2	53	38	34	39	14	267	378	26	97	.961
1947	153	.273	549	150	26	9	2	78	60	57	31	11	340	450	25	111	.969
1948	128	.252	464	117	13	2	6	65	50	60	24	6	259	348	17	85	.973
1949	153	.275	614	169	22	7	5	110	64	72	34	18	329	440	23	118	.971
1950	155	.324	617	200	36	7	7	125	66	92	38	12	301	452	14	13	.982
1951	144	.274	540	148	21	6	2	87	43	58	27	18	317	407	24	113	.968
1952	152	.254	578	147	24	10	2	89	43	67	42	18	308	458	19	115	.976
1953	134	.271	413	112	21	3	2	54	54	71	39	17	214	409	24	100	.963
1954	127	.195	307	60	11	0	1	47	15	41	23	4	185	294	16	84	.968
1955	81	.259	143	37	4	1	1	19	9	22	18	3	93	132	10	30	.957
1956	31	.231	52	12	0	0	0	6	6	6	6	3	31	54	6	17	.934
13 yrs.	1661	.273	5816	1588	239	62	38	877	562	651	397	149	3220	4666	263	1217	.968

Pee Wee Reese
Career Stats

Year	Games	BA	AB	H	2B	3B	HR	R	RBI	BB	SO	SB	PO	A	E	DP	FA
1940	84	.272	312	85	8	4	5	58	28	45	42	15	190	238	18	41	.960
1941	152	.229	595	136	23	5	2	76	46	68	56	10	346	473	47	76	.946
1942	151	.255	564	144	24	5	3	87	53	82	55	15	337	482	35	99	.959
1946	152	.284	542	154	16	10	5	79	60	87	71	10	285	463	26	104	.966
1947	142	.284	476	135	24	4	12	81	73	104	67	7	266	441	25	99	.966
1948	151	.274	566	155	31	4	9	96	75	79	63	25	335	453	31	93	.962
1949	155	.279	617	172	27	3	16	132	73	116	59	26	316	454	18	93	.977
1950	141	.260	531	138	21	5	11	97	52	91	62	17	291	414	26	95	.964
1951	154	.286	616	176	20	8	10	94	84	81	57	20	292	422	35	106	.953
1952	149	.272	559	152	18	8	6	94	58	86	59	30	282	376	21	89	.969
1953	140	.271	524	142	25	7	13	108	61	82	61	22	265	380	23	83	.966
1954	141	.309	554	171	35	8	10	98	69	90	62	8	270	426	25	74	.965
1955	145	.282	553	156	29	4	10	99	61	78	60	8	239	404	23	86	.965
1956	147	.257	572	147	19	2	9	85	46	56	69	13	269	388	25	80	.963
1958	59	.224	147	33	7	2	4	21	17	26	15	1	44	89	10	16	.930
16 yrs.	2166	.269	8058	2170	330	80	126	1338	885	1210	890	232	4124	6131	407	1255	.962

often while active that the election of Reese to the Hall of Fame has created a widespread assumption that Rizzuto must follow.

"While Rizzuto might well have been a great player, strong evidence for this does not survive in the statistics; the case for Reese is much better. Rizzuto won an MVP award, but that was in part because he had one season, the 1950 season, that was way above his head. Reese never had any such season, but finished among the top ten in the MVP voting eight times, which to me is a much more impressive accomplishment.

"Reese's defensive stats are a little better. It's kind of a B-plus against a B, actually, with (Lou) Boudreau and (Marty) Marion being the A students. Reese's offensive stats are quite a bit better."

It looked, for a long time, as if neither Rizzuto nor Reese would be elected to the Hall of Fame. Neither garnered enough support during his initial 15-year eligibility period, when the baseball writers make the selections, and later, both were by-passed by the Veterans Committee. In 1972, near the end of their 15-year eligibility period (Reese was eligible through 1978; Rizzuto through 1976), Rizzuto said, "I'm disappointed. But my skin just gets thicker over the years. Pee Wee and I seem to be going backwards in the voting. I guess we'll wind up being considered by the Old Timers' group."

In the spring of 1984, well past the initial 15-year period, as Rizzuto was driving to a Yankee exhibition game, he listened on his car radio as it was announced that Pee Wee Reese and . . . Rick Ferrell were selected by the Veterans Committee to be inducted into the Hall of Fame. Rizzuto's life flashed before him as he waited for the second name to be announced. "Could it be?" he wondered. Everyone had always said that when one goes in, so will the other. "Oh God, I've made it, too," he said to himself.

When Ferrell's name came beaming through the speaker, Rizzuto nearly drove off the road. This time, it really, really hurt. "I actually considered staying in Florida with the retired folks," he was quoted as saying a few days later. "I was really down in the dumps about the whole situation." Knowing how this rejection in particular bothered him, his four children, one by one, phoned to say how much they loved him, how much they cared for him, how he was in their Hall of Fame. It was the only thing that kept him going that spring.

He would claim years later that 1984 was the only year he was truly disappointed about not getting in. "I figured we might go in together," Rizzuto said of Reese and himself. But it was not to be that year, and more and more it is doubtful Rizzuto will ever get in.

Reese was as surprised as Phil when he got in and Rizzuto did not. "I always thought he was one of the greatest shortstops I ever played with, or had ever seen. When they said I was going in the Hall of Fame I kind of thought Phil would be going in, too. I don't know what the story is there. People ask me why Phil isn't in and I really don't know. I'm not a judge of that. I wish Phil were there, too. I don't know whether he had done something (to anger the voters).

"Myself, I never thought I'd be going into the Hall of Fame. I always thought the Hall of Fame was for the Ruths, the Gehrigs, the Musials, the superstars. I never looked at myself as a superstar. But Lefty Gomez said to me one day, 'Pee Wee, it doesn't matter how you get in. Be it the front door, the back door, the side door, or through the chimney, as long as you get in there. I'm very proud to be there. I wish Phil were there, but I don't know the reasons why he is not."

Actually, what is lost in the shuffle here is that, in truth, Rizzuto never came close to being elected to the Hall of Fame in any of the 13 years he was originally eligible. It is 13 years because, up until 1966, the baseball writers selected Hall of Famers every other year, with the Veterans Committee voting every year (over the years the Veterans Committee had sporadically voted in new members, but since 1961, it has voted in new members in every year except two—1988 and 1993).

Rizzuto first became eligible for the Hall in 1962, a full five years after he was let go by the Yankees. In his first year of eligibility, a year when Bob Feller, Bill McKechnie, Jackie Robinson, and Edd Roush were selected, Rizzuto received just 44 votes. Throughout his remaining years of eligibility, his vote total increased each year (with the exception of 1974, when he matched 1973's total of 111 votes; however, the percentage of votes needed varied) but never came close to the required 75% of the votes as the table on the following page indicates.

Votes	Votes needed	Percentage
1962 — 44	120	37
1964 — 45	151	30
1966 — 54	227	24
1967 — 71	219	32
1968 — 74	212	35
1969 — 78	255	30
1970 — 79	225	35
1971 — 92	270	34
1972 — 103	297	35
1973 — 111	285	39
1974 — 111	274	40
1975 — 117	272	43
1976 — 149	291	51

His highest vote total came in 1976, his final year of eligibility, when he amassed 149, good for ninth place. However, he would have needed 291 votes for election. In 1964, the year in which Luke Appling was elected to the Hall of Fame, Rizzuto was one of 30 former players who were in a runoff election after no one had garnered enough votes in the first tally. Rizzuto received just 11 votes the second time. In the last runoff vote in 1967, Rizzuto gained only 14 votes.

Since his eligibility with the Veterans Committee, beginning in 1982, he has received very little support. Although the voting is kept secret, Rizzuto has reportedly never gotten more than five votes among the 18 (currently there are only 15 active) members, which include former players, executives, writers, and broadcasters.

The committee consists of Charles Segar, Bob Broeg, Buck O'Neil, Jack Brickhouse, Al Lopez, Stan Musial, Ted Williams, Allen Lewis, Edgar Munzel, Shirley Povich, Joe L. Brown, Buzzie Bavasi, Ernie Harwell, Gabe Paul, Monte Irvin, and Roy Campanella (Campanella has not attended a meeting in years and likely will be replaced this summer). For Rizzuto to gain induction via the Veterans Committee, he would need to garner at least 75% of the vote. He is always good for a handful of votes, but no more.

Rizzuto, so upset with his Hall of Fame status, vowed he would never visit Cooperstown. However, in the summer of 1992, days after Seaver was inducted into the Hall of Fame along with Rollie Fingers, Hal Newhouser, and Bill McGowan, Rizzuto finally made the trek to the picturesque village in upstate New York. He was in Cooperstown to sign autographs at a store in town.

Rizzuto and his wife Cora fully expected to check in one day, sign autographs, maybe play a round of golf, then check out the next day. Bill Guilfoile, a former Yankee assistant public relations director and now the associate director of the National Baseball Hall of Fame, bumped into the Rizzutos as they unloaded the luggage from their car at the hotel.

"I bumped into Phil on the street," recalls Guilfoile. "He was up there to do an autograph show. He was unloading his car and I told him that if he wanted a tour of the hall to let me know. He told me, 'I promised myself that I'd never come until I was elected.' But the next morning, I get in, and who left a message? Phil. He and his wife Cora came over that morning, and I thought they really enjoyed themselves. He looked at the various exhibits and saw his shoes and glove on display. And, of course, he's in so many photographs because of his playing with the Yankees."

Interestingly, Rizzuto insists that the glove on display is not his. He has no idea whose glove it is. The shoes, he concedes, could be his. The shoes, and glove, whomever it belongs to, are permanent fixtures at the Hall of Fame. Is this as close as Rizzuto will get into the Hall of Fame? A short visit? Time is not on his side.

Rizzuto's good friend, former *Kansas City Star* sportswriter Sid Bordman, also swore he would never visit the Hall of Fame, in defiance of Scooter's omission. "That Hall of Fame thing is a sore spot with me." Bordman says, "I have a vote in it, and of course, I can't vote for him any more. But I did when he was eligible (in the writers' voting). The year he should have gotten in was the year (Negro League star) Ray Dandridge got in."

That was 1987, the same year that Jim "Catfish" Hunter and Billy Williams were elected to the hall. Dandridge was picked by the Veterans Committee. "That was a joke," Bordman says. "I saw him play for Minneapolis. He was 30 years old then, so he wasn't over the hill. I didn't think much of him. It was a numbers game. I was going to wait to go to the hall until he got in, but I've sort of lost hope. I went up to the hall recently. I had never been there."

"I moved around," says Billy Hitchcock in his sweet-sounding southern drawl. "I went from Washington to St. Louis to Philadelphia. I saw Phil every time we played the Yankees. He turned out to be just what I thought he'd be. I'm really disappointed he's not in the Hall of Fame. He should be. That's my opinion. Boudreau was playing short at Cleveland, and of course, Lou was a fine shortstop—1948 was his best year. Vern Stephens was the shortstop at Boston at that time and he was a power hitter. But Phil was a good all-around shortstop. There were good shortstops around the league. I thought Phil was the outstanding shortstop."

"Why, if I had to be one to vote in the Hall of Fame, I'd say he'd be a Hall of Famer," notes Gil McDougald, who played alongside Rizzuto at third base and second base, and later replaced Scooter at shortstop. "But once again, a lot of times there's no criteria to make the Hall of Fame. And a lot of times it becomes a popularity contest. Also, once you've been out of baseball for a number of years like Phil, they seem to forget how really good he was."

"There is no doubt in my mind that he should be in the Hall of Fame," offers former Cleveland Indian manager and player Lou Boudreau, a Hall of Fame shortstop. "He was consistent. If there was anything against Phil, it was that he didn't hit the long ball and that's what a lot of sportswriters look for when they vote. They look for the long ball, the extra-base hits.

"But defense is an important part of the game and Phil could hold his own out there. He may not have had the long ball, but he did so many other things brilliantly that you overlook that. In different situations he would be capable of doing different things to hurt you. He would not always do the normal thing in a given situation. That's what made him so valuable. Unfortunately, the writers spent too much time looking at cold stats and nothing more."

"He was a hell of a ball player," adds former Indian hurler Bob Lemon, a Hall of Famer as well. "He did everything you could ask of a player. Field, run, hit. I don't know what's keeping him out of the Hall of Fame."

"Does he belong in the Hall of Fame?" asks Gene Hermanski, who played with the Brooklyn Dodgers for seven years. "Phil was a great shortstop. I played with Pee Wee and Pee Wee made it. I firmly believe that Phil should be in, too, because of that. You know, where would the Yankees have gone all those years without a good shortstop? Right? I believe Ted Williams said, 'If we had Rizzuto playing shortstop we would've won the pennant instead of the Yankees.'"

"He belongs in the Hall of Fame," emphasizes Bill White, who is on the Hall of Fame Board of Directors. "I'm not on the Veterans Committee. I might be once I get out of here (as league president). Let's just say there's politics in every phase of life. There shouldn't be, but unfortunately, there is. He needs somebody to push him, preferably someone on the committee."

Former Yankee great Tommy Henrich, an outfielder when Rizzuto first came up to the major leagues in 1941, can't figure out the Hall of Fame system, Rizzuto or otherwise.

"The thing that's hurting Phil is that the guys voting for the Hall of Fame don't give one doggone about defense. All right! For Heaven's sake, I would say half, more than half, of Rizzuto's value to the New York Yankees was for his defense. And yet, he was also known as a guy who could bunt like crazy, and he wasn't a bad hitter. He was by no means an embarrassment at home plate. He didn't have much power but he did get his base hits.

"But the Hall of Fame is based on one thing. They don't even discuss what value he had as a defensive man for the Yankees. And yet they put in slow-footed bums that are outfielders that hit 400 homers and they waltz in the front door. It's ridiculous. And they got guys who set records for strikeouts but because they hit home runs, they put them in. I have a very definite feeling about that type of voting.

"There are a lot of guys on my list who should be in. Like who would you rather have on your team, nine Bill Mazeroskis or nine Ralph Kiners? Mazeroski played both ways. Same thing about Phil. I don't know how to put it, but I think you get the idea. With all this noise for this many years, he's pretty frustrated."

"To inject some of my thoughts about the Hall of Fame, a bunch of those Dodgers were elected to the Hall of Fame, guys we beat every year!" declares former Yankee hurler Allie Reynolds.

"It's hard to understand the thoughts of the voters. The Dodgers had great ball clubs. I know that. But they didn't win any of the series I played in. We won them all. An editor once asked me, 'What do you think of them putting all those Dodgers in the Hall of Fame?' I said, 'You can't blame it on us.'"

"There's a lot of guys in Phil's category," notes Woodling. "Every guy has his opinion. The guy I think should be in the Hall of Fame is Mickey Vernon. He was buried down in Washington."

Even former New York Giant Bobby Thomson, whose "Shot Heard 'Round the World" made history in 1951, says, "I didn't see him that much, but they wouldn't have won without him. You've got to figure he's got as much right as some of these other fellas that have made it."

About the only former player who is vehemently against Rizzuto getting into the Hall of Fame is long-time Rizzuto nemesis Eddie Stanky. Days after Rizzuto was passed over in the spring of 1987, Stanky said, "I'm glad Rizzuto didn't make it. He didn't deserve it. He was a crybaby and not that good a ball player."

Rizzuto surely would love to join his Yankee teammates who have been enshrined. Bill Dickey, Red Ruffing, and Lefty Gomez were there at the start of Rizzuto's career, and Joe DiMaggio, Yogi Berra, Whitey Ford, and Mickey Mantle came later. Two of Rizzuto's managers, Joe McCarthy and Casey Stengel, are in the hall, too. According to many, Phil should be there as well.

There has been some talk over the years that perhaps Rizzuto has a better chance of making the Hall of Fame as a broadcaster. Rizzuto himself downplays this possibility of receiving the Frick Award, given to broadcasters. Several times he has said that he wouldn't want to make it that way, that he doesn't consider himself a professional announcer. He is the first to admit that his style behind the mike is not the accepted norm.

As a footnote, those broadcasters inducted into the Hall of Fame are not actually in the hall. Instead, broadcasters and writers (Spink Award) have a section in the media wing of the Hall of Fame library.

Making the Hall of Fame as a player is not a likely prospect for Phil Rizzuto, although I for one, have come to believe that Rizzuto surely does belong with the game's greatest ball players.

When I first began writing this book, I was neutral about whether Phil Rizzuto should be enshrined in Baseball's Hall of Fame. I'd heard all the barking by George Steinbrenner, and others, that Rizzuto deserved to be in the Hall of Fame. Steinbrenner, who loves Rizzuto and would do anything for him, has often spoke out for Rizzuto and makes no bones of his belief that a great injustice has been perpetrated here.

No matter what Steinbrenner, or others, said however, I was not sold on the idea of Phil being in the hall. I looked at his numbers. Nothing special, really. Fairly good hitter, fine fielder. But nothing jumps out at you.

The more I read, though, the more I spoke to people, the more I realized how much Phil Rizzuto does deserve to be in the Hall of Fame. Okay, so his numbers don't match up with a lot of other Hall of Famers. So what? His numbers DO compare favorably to a majority of the shortstops that are already in, and his seven world championships far surpass any other shortstop.

And keep in mind, the one offensive category where Rizzuto could have rung up some huge numbers was in the stolen base department. Phil was fast. Very fast. In this day and age, his 149 career stolen bases could have translated into four times, maybe five times, the amount. That puts him right up there with the all-time great base stealers. Obviously, with those big Yankee sticks, he didn't have to steal 50 bases a year. Had he, his opponents would have cried foul. Unlike these days, you just didn't steal for the heck of it back then. The days of swiping bases with a four or five run lead a la Rickey Henderson or Vince Coleman, were still decades away.

In the field, he did not have the greatest arm, yet there is no question his fielding ability puts him among the best, although Yogi Berra, for one, points out that Astroturf might have been a problem for his friend today. "They look for guys with good arms now because they have to play deeper," Yogi points out. "But you know," he adds, "he never missed on the dirt; he might not have missed any on Astroturf, where the bounce is truer."

Adds Lou Boudreau, "I think he would have been fine on Astroturf simply because of his speed and quick movements." As for Phil, he simply stated to Joe Calabrese of the *Newark Star-Ledger*, "Baseball was meant to be played on grass. Turf cheapened the game."

Most important, however, Phil Rizzuto is one of those ball players who deserves to be in the Hall of Fame by virtue of his intangibles. How many times do you hear someone say, "You can't win a pennant without a good shortstop"? Well, Phil played on nine major league pennant winners, and four more in the minors.

With Phil starting at short, New York won seven world championships, including that incredible string from 1949 to 1953, when the Yankees won five straight World Series. You can argue that the Yankees might have won all those championships with any old shortstop, but I doubt it. One of the main reasons the Yankees won all those flags was Rizzuto's consistent play in the field, and at the plate.

Is it Rizzuto's fault that he was overshadowed by so many other big stars? Rizzuto's chances of getting into the Hall of Fame do not seem good. But as long as there is a glimmer of hope, let that glimmer keep shining. Keep the faith, Phil.

"Stand up a minute, Phil."
"I am standing up."

—Phil Rizzuto, responding to a fan as he stood in the Yankee Stadium stands before a game. Associated Press.

▪ 12 ▪

Reflections

"Rizzuto: Two-Way Vet on Field and on Air"
by Phil Rizzuto

*Reprinted with permission from
The Sporting News, April 1976.*

NEW YORK—The year after I collected my last World Series check, I became a rookie all over again—a broadcasting rookie.

It was 1957. It was a lot easier than 1941. You see, the spring and summer of '41 was my introduction to the Yankees, to the stadium, to the greatest thing in baseball. And even if I came in as the "Minor League Player of the Year," nobody accepted me on my press clippings.

No, sir. Not the Yankees. I was, in their eyes, just a busher. I was the guy who was supposed to take Frank Crosetti's job. They all loved the Crow. So they resented me. That's the way it was as a baseball rookie and it wasn't until mid-June, when I got my average over .300, that Joe DiMaggio started kidding me. I was very naive, the perfect foil for the practical jokers. And when DiMaggio got into the act, that broke the ice.

Broadcasting was almost a lark. I mean, the start-in period. In the first place, I broke in with two of the greatest pros of all time, Mel Allen and Red Barber. Then, too, I had a taste of it even when I wore the Yankee uniform.

My last year or two as a Yankee, Casey Stengel would pinch-hit for me occasionally and I'd hustle into my street clothes and run up to the broadcast booth. Mel or Red would let me do a half inning or so. I tried it and I liked it. That's what set me off.

So in 1957 I went from the field to the booth, and it all seemed so easy. I'd do one inning on radio, the third, and another inning on television, the seventh, and it seemed like a breeze.

But I'll never forget the second week of spring training games in St. Petersburg. The Yankees and Cardinals were about to get one started when the rain came. This was radio only and I started to get up when Mel said: "Phil, I'm gonna get a hot dog with Red. We'll be right back. You take it."

So that's how they force-fed me. They didn't come back for 15 minutes. I mean, they were off in a corner where they could see and hear me, but they made me fill that dead air unassisted. That's the toughest part of broadcasting. Filling the dead air. Keeping your audience, amusing them, when things are not happening. That first time, in St. Pete, I was in a state of shock. By the time the regular season started, I was ready for it.

There's a lot to broadcasting that may not seem obvious to the listener. To my way of thinking, one of the most important assets anybody in the booth can have is the ability to pick up the ball as soon as it leaves the bat. The good broadcaster reacts before the crowd. He may not always be right, but at least he doesn't let the crowd lead him. He informs before the background noises tip off the audience.

This was one of Mel Allen's strongest suits. He could build up the drama of a play because he sensed that it was going to be tough but playable. And quite often, with a Yankee team that grabbed everything in sight, he was anticipating great plays.

Some broadcasters try to cover up that deficiency with some preliminary words, like, "He swings." Everybody can see the batter swing, but they'll say it anyway just to give themselves more time to pick up the flight of the ball.

One thing about Mel Allen though. He was very superstitious. He grew up in the baseball ideology that says you never mention a pitcher is working on a no-hitter. I remember one game in my rookie year. They gave me the seventh inning and as soon as I got to the mike, I said Whitey Ford still hadn't given up a hit. Mel Allen almost jumped out of the booth.

I couldn't understand that. Neither could Red Barber. But Mel wasn't going to tell Red how to broadcast, or vice versa. With me, it was different.

"You just don't do that," Allen would say.

"But how is the audience supposed to know?" I'd react, "Suppose they tuned in late?"

Allen was superstitious in other ways. If Mickey Mantle was 3-for-3 and now he was up a fourth time with a chance to drive in the tying and winning runs, Mel would never tell the audience that Mantle already had a perfect day. That would be jinxing him. Mel rooted in a way that could only be described as "reverse English." He would build up the opposition before the fact, the Yankees only after the fact.

But he was a perfectionist and he taught me a lot. I used to say somebody hit a foul ball back in the stands. And Mel would say: "Back where? Tell 'em it's behind the plate, or behind first, or wherever."

At the same time, in the interest of fair play, the playing conditions should be noted if they are a factor. Maybe it's that time between daylight and night ball. The lights could be on without taking effect. You can't rip a player. But you don't cover up, either.

I heard one call on the air waves recently. It was radio. The hitter drove one down the right field line and would end up on second. The call made it sound like a clean double. Then the broadcaster said, "Make it a single and an error." Seems the outfielder fumbled the ball. Well, if he did, the audience should have been let in before the official scorer put an error on the board.

I also think that statistics can be a big bore if they're overdone. I'd rather talk about the weather, or a movie I caught up with. Baseball is a fun game and it is meant to be controversial.

That's why it is so easy to enjoy. No two teams are ever alike. I might see something even now, after 40 years in the game, that I never saw before. Or hear something.

The other night, (Yankee announcer) Frank Messer said to me, "Didja know if a player throws lefthanded, the left eye is the dominant eye?"

I said I didn't know. I asked him how he knew. He said he read it in a medical journal. Well, I don't read those things any more than Yogi Berra. And if I did, I wouldn't believe it. I always thought the dominant eye was the eye up front. If you bat left, it's the right eye that's dominant.

So I did my own checking, and one of these days, I'm going to have some fun with Frank Messer. After all, that's what baseball and broadcasting are all about. Fun.

Red Barber was equally fastidious about his work. He'd always get on me to improve my English. If I said I had a pizza pie before the ball game, he'd say that was redundant. "Pizza," Barber said, "means pie." How was I to know? I'm very weak with the Italian language.

I always enjoyed working with Barber because he'd ask me questions about baseball that were purely meant to draw me out. He knew the answers. He just wanted the audience to hear it from me. That's a good man.

There were times, also, when I might sense something he did not. For instance, I remember seeing Billy Martin take a lead off third base and measure the pitcher for a steal of home. It was a big ball game and I whispered over to Red that it could happen right there. Well, instead of calling the play a possibility himself, Red said: "Here, Phil, you take the mike." And I came off smelling like roses.

But then I can also remember times when Red would read something that morning and try me out for size. Like, he'd find out what is the natural rock for the state of Michigan, or how many states are on the Nevada border. Now, how was I supposed to answer that?

But that's what I mean about dead air, and a guy in the business of broadcasting ball games has to keep the flow of the game from running dry.

It's important also to be as natural as possible. I want to see the Yankees win, but I don't want to hide anything from the audience. If somebody doesn't get to a ball, if I think he should have got to it, I won't rant and rave, but I might suggest he broke too slowly. Nobody wants to be accused of being a house man. There must be loyalty to the listener.

"My whole life I've been a Yankee. I'm doing the Yankee games. I'm paid by the Yankees. I'm not told what to say and what not to say by the owners. If the other team makes an outstanding play, I don't think I hit as high a decibel, but I'm fair."

—*Phil Rizzuto, Inside Sports*

————— • **13** • —————

"It's Sports Time!"

"It's Sports Time with Phil Rizzuto"
January 12, 1966
(Reprinted with permission from CBS)

Announcer: "It's Sports Time with Phil Rizzuto" is presented by Winston cigarettes. Now, here is Phil Rizzuto:

RIZZUTO: Hi, everybody! In my prejudiced opinion, no other sport can quite match baseball's Hall of Fame. From that day in 1936 when the game's historians—the Baseball Writers Association—elected as charter members five former greats . . . Ty Cobb . . . Babe Ruth . . . Christy Mathewson . . . Honus Wagner and Walter Johnson (in that order) many have been called but comparatively few chosen!

About this time each year the writers review the list and make their selections, narrowing their final choice to as few as one or as many as six. With each ballot having space for 10 names, if none should rate the required 75% vote, nobody gets in. It's happened, 1958 being the last blank year. Concerning the game's great old-timers, they are voted in by a special committee of directors. As things stand now, the moderns come up for scrutiny on the even year while the old-timers swing on the odd year. This year being an even one, the bells are ringing for Ted Williams, who has now been out of the game for the mandatory five-year period. Ted's lifetime batting average of .344 is surpassed by but three batsmen of this century: Cobb, Hornsby, and Shoeless Joe Jackson. Concerning home runs, despite five of his most productive years being spent as a marine flier in two wars, Williams hit 521 as compared to the Babe's all-time mark of 714. Where Ruth put in 21 years, Ted had only 16 full seasons. Certainly, off his slugging alone, it would seem that Theodore Samuel Williams rates full induction honors when those Saints Go Marching In next July.

In his recent year-in-sport forecast wherein *New York Times* writer Arthur Daley rubs the old crystal ball, when he got to July he wrote: "The Hall of Fame directors, ignoring rules and showing unexpected common sense, vote Casey Stengel and Branch Rickey into the Cooperstown shrine." By rights, I suppose, Stengel and the late Rickey might be considered old-timers, which means they would have to wait until '67. Also, in as much as Rickey was never a great player, but rather an administrator, there is some question as to his validity for enshrinement under current rules . . . which, I understand, will be reviewed next summer! Whatever their subsequent action, if those directors should run a red light and enshrine both men, it would be a ten-strike with the fans. That being the case, I'd like to offer another "name" for consideration. (Pause) I mean the late and great Grantland Rice.

But more about that after this message from our sponsor.

Commercial: Winston

RIZZUTO: From the year 1900, when he graduated from Vanderbilt University and picked up a typewriter rather than accept a tryout from the Chicago White Sox . . . to his death in 1954, Grantland Rice accomplished more positive good for the game than any picket line of .300 hitters . . . or 20-game winners! Granny came along when Cobb was a bush minor leaguer looking for a write-up. Granny gave it to him . . . which helped Detroit to uncover Cobb in 1905, where as a social outcast he hit .240 in 41 games. P.S. He never hit less than .320 in his subsequent 23 seasons!

Cobb . . . Napoleon Lajoie . . . Rube Marquand . . . Shoeless Joe Jackson—from the stars of the early 1900s clear down to the Mickey Mantles of the '50s, Rice covered them with a special kind of glory that did more to popularize the game and the big gate than the players themselves!

Baseball's Hall of Fame?

Now dead these past 11 years, Grantland Rice deserves his niche up there with those he did so much to create!
And that's the sports picture for now. This is Phil Rizzuto saying good night.

Commercial: Guardian Maintenance

Announcer: Listen in tomorrow night when "It's Sports Time with Phil Rizzuto" is brought to you by General Motors for Guardian Maintenance Service.

NOTE: Ted Williams and Casey Stengel were elected to the Hall of Fame in 1966. Williams was chosen by the Baseball Writers Association, with Stengel being elected at the urging of the writers who implored the Veterans Committee to make a special case to elect Stengel, since he was in ill health and was not expected to live much longer. Stengel had the last laugh, however, living until 1975. Similar exceptions to the rule were incorporated with the election of Lou Gehrig and Roberto Clemente. Also in 1966, Grantland Rice garnered the J. G. Taylor Spink Award, which honors sportswriters "for meritorious contributions to baseball writing." Branch Rickey was elected to the Hall of Fame in 1967.

Index

Allen, Maury, 144
Allen, Mel, 47, 128, 135, 137, 138, 139, 140, 183, 185
Amoros, Sandy, 122, 123
Anderson, Arnold, 45
Aparicio, Luis, 167
Appel, Marty, 72, 140, 141, 146
Appling, Luke, 48, 167, 174
Arcaro, Eddie, 105
Avila, Bobby, 119, 131

Bancroft, Dave, 167
Banks, Ernie, 167
Barber, Red, 137, 138, 139, 140, 183, 186
Barrow, Ed, 12, 28, 32, 45
Bauer, Hank, 95, 103, 109, 110, 111, 112, 119, 121, 126
Bavasi, Buzzie, 174
Baylor, Don, 165
Beazley, Johnny, 77
Benzenberg, Ralph, 5, 7
Berberet, Lou, 125
Berra, Yogi, 87, 90, 98, 100, 102, 103, 111, 112, 114, 119, 121, 122, 124, 126, 127, 128, 132, 143, 158, 165, 178, 179
Bevens, Bill, 89
Blomberg, Ron, 145
Boland, William, 105
Bonanno, Angelo, 153, 154, 156
Bonham, Ernie, 42
Bordagaray, Frenchy, 54
Bordman, Sid, 19, 30, 152, 175
Boudreau, Lou, 48, 76, 97, 108, 115, 131, 167, 172, 176, 179
Boyle, Buzz, 19
Bradley, Bill, 163
Branca, Ralph, 88, 90, 109, 158
Brickhouse, Jack, 174
Broeg, Bob, 174
Brown, Bobby, 82, 84, 87, 99, 100, 108, 110, 113, 131, 151
Brown, Joe, 174
Byrd, Harry, 120
Byrne, Tommy, 98, 99, 122, 129

Calabrese, Joe, 179
Campanella, Roy, 99, 102, 122, 123, 174
Candini, Milo, 78
Carew, Rod, 165
Carey, Andy, 110, 113, 118, 119, 128, 138, 168
Carrasquel, Chico, 108, 112
Carson, Harry, 163
Case, George, 63
Casey, Hugh, 57, 78
Chandler, Happy, 88
Chandler, Spud, 38, 81
Cerdan, Marcel, 105
Cerone, Rick, 146
Chambliss, Chris, 144
Chase, Ken, 66
Clark, Allie, 131
Clemente, Roberto, 191
Cobb, Ty, 52, 189, 190
Coleman, Jerry, 90, 96, 98, 99, 100, 110, 117, 121, 128, 139, 169
Collins, Joe, 111, 112, 119, 122, 124
Combs, Earle, 51
Cooper, Mort, 77
Cooper, Walker, 26
Corbitt, Claude, 18
Coscarart, Pete, 56
Cronin, Joe, 43, 94, 167
Crosetti, Frank, 34, 35, 36, 37, 41, 47, 49, 50, 51, 54, 63, 64, 65, 66, 67, 68, 81, 82, 132, 183

Daniel, Dan, 11, 29, 36, 37 38, 39, 84, 104, 126, 127
Dahlgren, Babe, 37
Dandridge, Ray, 175
Dark, Al, 109, 169
Delaney, Bob, 136
Dent, Bucky, 144
Dickey, Bill, 33, 34, 35, 38, 40, 57, 62, 80, 83, 165, 178
DiMaggio, Dom, 76, 97
DiMaggio, Joe, 10, 23, 33, 35, 37, 40, 42, 50, 51, 52, 53, 55, 56, 57, 83, 87, 88, 91, 92, 95, 96, 98, 100, 103, 104, 106,

DiMaggio, Joe, cont. 110, 115, 124, 127, 145, 165, 178, 183
DiMaggio, Vince, 22
Dixon, John "Sonny", 129
Doby, Larry, 88, 102, 104, 119, 163
Doerr, Bobby, 76, 102
Donald, Atley, 42
Dressen, Charley, 88, 120
Dresser, Betty, 74
Dropo, Walt, 102, 104
Durocher, Leo, 54, 55, 56, 88, 109, 158, 159

Erskine, Carl, 113
Estalella, Roberto, 19
Evers, Hoot, 102

Farrell, John, 137
Feller, Bob, 48, 52, 66, 78, 119, 173
Ferrell, Rick, 172
Fingers, Rollie, 175
Fitzsimmons, Fred, 56
Fletcher, Art, 49, 67
Ford, Whitey, 100, 104, 119, 121, 125, 128, 150, 165, 168
Franks, Herman, 110
Frick, Ford, 140
Frisch, Frankie, 136
Froelich, Eddie, 32, 33
Furillo, Carl, 88, 122, 123

Gamere, Bob, 139
Garagiola, Joe, 139, 140, 141
Garcia, Mike, 101, 119, 131
Gaven, Michael, 119, 123
Gehrig, Lou, 10, 76, 165, 173, 191
Gibbs, Jake, 145
Goetz, Larry, 55
Gomez, Lefty, 33, 35, 40, 42, 45, 60, 61, 173, 178
Goodman, Billy, 104
Goodman, Murray, 105
Gordon, Joe, 31, 34, 36, 57, 62, 63, 64, 66, 67, 76, 77, 80, 87
Goren, Herbert, 46, 47
Gowdy, Curt, 139
Grande, George, 139
Grieve, Bill, 55
Grim, Bob, 119

Gromek, Steve, 101
Gross, Milton, 48
Grove, Lefty, 70
Guilfoile, Bill, 150, 175

Halberstam, David, 43
Harris, Bucky, 90, 93
Harwell, Ernie, 174
Head, Ed, 42
Healy, Fran, 139, 141
Held, Woody, 118
Henrich, Tommy, 33, 36, 38, 49, 69, 76, 86, 94, 95, 98, 99, 100, 106, 131, 177
Herman, Billy, 56
Hermanski, Gene, 89, 114, 158
Herzog, Whitey, 125
Hickock Award, 105, 106, 126, 163, 169
Hitchcock, Billy, 19, 20, 23, 34, 76, 169, 176
Hodges, Gil, 99, 122, 123
Hodges, Russ, 136
Hogan, Ben, 105
Holmes, Tommy, 12
Howard, Elston, 76, 122, 124, 142, 165
Hubbell, Carl, 38
Hunter, Billy, 120
Hunter, Jim "Catfish", 175
Hutchinson, Freddy, 79

Irvin, Monte, 174

Jackson, Shoeless Joe, 190
Jackson, Travis, 167
James, Bill, 169
Jennings, Hugh, 167
Johnson, Walter, 189
Joost, Eddie, 97, 101, 102

Kaat, Jim, 139
Keeler, Willie, 52, 53
Kell, George, 102, 104
Keller, Charlie, 34, 37, 41, 42, 55, 57, 77
Keltner, Ken, 76
Kekich, Mike, 145
Kiner, Ralph, 102, 177
Kline, Bob, 125
Koch, Ed, 155
Koenig, Mark, 10
Konstanty, Jim, 105

Koslo, Dave, 108, 109
Krichell, Paul, 10, 13, 15, 131
Kubek, Tony, 126
Kucks, Johnny, 128, 132, 138, 143
Kunitz, Al, 5, 6, 7
Kuzava, Bob, 111

Labine, Clem, 127
La joie, Napoleon,190
LaMotta, Jake, 105, 106
Landis, Kenesaw Mountain, 31
Lane, Frank,130
Lanier, Hal, 145
Larsen, Don, 120, 126, 130
Lavagetto, Cookie, 89
Lazzeri, Tony, 10, 11, 34, 169
Lindell, Johnny, 19, 34, 86, 98
Lindsay, Ted, 105
Lemon, Bob, 103, 104, 107, 119, 176
Leonard, Dutch, 66
Lewis, Allen, 174
Lodigiani, Dario,68, 69
Logan, Bob,26
Logan, Fred, 33
Lopat, Ed, 98, 108, 128, 129
Lopez, Al, 174
Lordi, Al, 153
Louis, Joe, 55
Lucas, Ed, 157, 158, 159, 160, 161
Lumpe, Jerry, 126
Lyons, Ted, 66

Mack, George, 10
MacPhail, Larry, 54, 81, 82, 84, 85, 86
Mantle, Mickey,108,110,111,112,113,
    118, 119, 121, 126, 164, 165, 178,
    185, 190
Maranville, Rabbit, 166, 167
Marion, Marty, 77, 102, 131, 172
Maris, Roger,144, 165
Marquand, Rube, 190
Martin, Billy,92,100,103,111,112,113,
    122, 124, 129, 139, 165, 186
Mathewson, Christy, 189
Mays, Willie, 164
Mazeroski, Bill, 177
McCarthy, Joe, 34, 36, 37, 38, 41, 43, 47,
    48, 49, 50, 51, 54, 58, 62, 63, 65, 66,
    68, 69, 70, 82, 94, 178

McDermott, Mickey, 95, 125, 129
McDonald, Jim, 120
McDougald, Gil, 108, 109, 112, 113,
    121, 122, 123, 124, 125, 126, 129,
    176
McGowan, Bill, 55, 175
McGuire, Dick, 105
McKechnie, Bill, 173, 185
Messer, Frank, 139, 142, 185, 186
Meyer, Bill, 19, 20
Mikan, George, 105
Miller, Eddie, 46, 48
Miller, Otto, 8, 9
Milosevich, Mike, 81
Miranda, Willie, 117, 118, 120
Mize, Johnny,76, 80, 99, 100, 101, 103,
    111, 169
Moore, John, 116, 141, 146, 149, 151
Morgan, Chet, 26
Morgan, Tom, 110
Munson, Thurman, 165
Munzel, Edgar, 174
Murcer, Bobby, 139, 141, 143, 145, 164,
    165
Murphy, Johnny, 57
Murray,Ray, 101
Musial, Stan, 77, 102, 173, 174

Newhouser, Hal, 175
Nokes, Matt, 166
Nova, Lou, 55

Ogle, Jim, 16, 17, 115, 125, 130, 168
Olmo, Luis, 99
O'Malley, Walter, 137
O'Neil, Buck, 174
Ott, Mel, 76
Owen, Mickey, 57, 76, 123

Paige, Satchel, 6,8
Pafko, Andy, 102
Page, Joe, 89, 95, 97, 99
Palmer, Jim, 156
Parnell, Mel, 96
Parrott, Harold, 88
Pasquel, Bernardo, 85
Pasquel, Jorge, 84
Patterson Arthur, 4, 29, 33, 112
Paul, Gabe, 174

Peckinpaugh, Roger, 51
Pepe, Phil, 130
Pesky, Johnny,95, 96
Pinelli, Babe, 55
Podres, Johnny, 122, 123
Prendergast, Jim, 12
Priddy, Gerry, 18, 20, 23, 26, 29, 30, 31,
    32, 34, 35, 36, 37, 41, 44, 46, 48, 49,
    50, 54, 66, 67, 68, 69, 78

Raschi, Vic, 98, 102, 104, 110, 111
Raynor, Chuck, 105
Reese, Pee Wee,32, 43, 46, 48, 56, 58, 78,
    79, 80, 88, 99, 102, 107, 111, 112,
    123,130,132,164,166,167,168,169,
    172, 176, 177
Reiser, Pete, 88
Reynolds, Allie, 87, 89, 95, 97, 98, 99,
    104, 108, 109, 110, 111, 113, 177
Rice, Grantland, 190, 191
Richardson, Bobby, 126
Rickey, Branch, 88, 191
Rizzuto, Cora, 74, 75, 78, 79, 80, 143,
    144, 159, 160, 168, 175
Rizzuto, Mary, 1
Rizzuto, Phil, Sr., 1, 15
Rizzuto, Rose, 1, 3, 17
Roberts, Robin, 102
Robinson, Eddie, 79
Robinson, Jackie, 99, 102, 123, 173
Robinson, Wilbert, 3
Roe, Preacher, 99
Rolfe, Red, 23, 37, 46, 55, 64, 66,68, 104
Roosevelt, Franklin D., 44, 45
Rosar, Buddy, 76
Rosen, Al, 119, 131, 173
Ross, Spencer, 139
Roush, Edd, 173
Rowe, Schoolboy, 80
Ruffing, Red, 33, 34, 35, 38, 40, 45, 62,
    77, 178
Russo, Marius, 6, 38, 45, 57
Ruth, Babe,87, 90,91,106,110,132,165,
    189, 190

Sain, Johnny, 129
Saltzgaver, Jack, 20
Sanderson, Scott, 164
Santagata, Lou, 155

Schillizzi, Anthony, 152, 153
Schulman, Arlene,146, 166
Seaver, Tom, 116, 139, 142, 143, 145,
    163, 164, 165, 166
Segar, Charles, 174
Selkirk, George, 38, 110
Sewell, Joe, 167
Shakoor, Charley,156
Shea, Spec, 89
Shotton, Burt, 88
Siebern, Norm, 129
Silvestri, Ken, 54
Sisler, George, 52
Skowron, Moose, 118, 122, 126, 127
Slaughter, Enos, "Country," 27, 99, 102,
    128, 129, 130
Smith, Hal, 120
Smith, Ozzie, 114
Snider, Duke, 111, 122, 123, 164
Snyder, Pancho, 10
Spiker, Calvin, 154, 155
Spink, J.G. Taylor, 135, 136, 138, 191
Stallard, Tracy, 144
Stankiewicz, Andy, 153
Stanky, Eddie, 109, 178
Steinbrenner, George, 92, 164, 179
Stengel, Casey, 8, 9, 93, 94, 101, 102,
    103, 110, 112, 115, 117, 118, 119,
    120, 121, 124, 125, 127, 135, 165,
    178, 183, 190, 191
Stephens, Vern, 97, 102, 176
Stirnweiss, George, 81, 112, 130
Sturm, Johnny, 23, 48, 49, 50, 55
Suder, Pete, 86
Sukeforth, Clyde, 88
Swift, Bob, 102

Taylor, Zach, 8
Tebbetts, Birdie, 76, 98
Thompson, Hank,88
Thomson, Bobby,90, 109, 157, 158
Tinker, Joe, 166, 167
Travis, Cecil, 46
Triandos, Gus, 120
Trimble, Joe, 8, 9, 15, 16, 45, 57, 74, 79,
    80, 101, 149
Trosky, Hal, 51
Turley, Bob, 121, 127

VanderMeer, Johnny, 26, 80
Vaughan, Arky, 167
Vernon, Mickey, 178
Villemain, Robert, 106

Wagner, Honus, 112, 167
Walker, Dixie, 88
Wallace, Bobby, 166, 167
Ward, Monte, 167
Webb, Del, 81
Weiss, George,119, 120, 126, 127, 129
Welch, James, 154
Wertz, Vic, 104
White, Bill, 92, 131, 139, 141, 142, 143, 145, 146, 155, 166, 175, 176, 177
White, Ernie, 77

White, Ray, 16
Williams, Bernie, 166
Williams, Joe, 31, 32
Williams, Ted, 44, 57, 76, 99, 102, 190, 191
Wilson, George, 129
Woodling, Gene, 86, 104, 110, 112, 113, 114, 120, 124, 168, 178
Wright, Ab, 26
Wyatt, Whitlow, 56
Wynn, Early, 119, 131

York, Rudy, 76
Yvars, Sal, 109, 151

Zuber, Bill, 78